Prayers
for

The Twelve Steps—
A Spiritual Journey

by Friends in Recovery
with Jerry S.

Prayers and Inspirational Readings
Written and Compiled by
Bill Pittman

RPI PUBLISHING, INC.

The Twelve Steps—
A Spiritual Journey

Published by
RPI Publishing, Inc.
P.O. Box 66398
Scotts Valley, CA 95067
(800) 873-8384

Library of Congress Cataloging-in-Publication Data
Prayers for the Twelve Steps: A Spiritual Journey / Friends in Recovery
& Jerry S.; prayers and inspirational readings written & compiled by Bill Pittman.
p.   cm.
ISBN 978-0-941405-28-7   (pbk.)
  1. Recovering addicts—Prayer-books and devotions—English.
  1. Jerry S.   II. Pittman, Bill 1947 -   III. Friends in Recovery.
BL624.5.P73   1993
242'.4-dc20   93-15978
                                                          CIP

The Twelve Steps are reprinted and adapted with permission of Alcoholics
Anonymous World Services, Inc. Permission to reprint and adapt this material
does not mean that AA has reviewed or approved the contents of this publication,
nor that AA agrees with the views expressed herein. AA is a program of recovery
from alcoholism only—use of the Twelve Steps in connection with programs and
activities which are patterned after AA, but which address other problems, does
not imply otherwise.

Scripture quotations marked (NIV) are from the Holy Bible, New International
Version. Copyright © 1973, 1978, 1984 International Bible Society. Used by
permission of Zondervan Bible Publishers.

Printed in the United States of America
First edition

Table of Contents

The Twelve Steps of Alcoholics Anonymous*

STEP ONE: We admitted we were powerless over alcohol—that our lives had become unmanageable.

STEP TWO: Came to believe in a Power greater than ourselves could restore us to sanity.

STEP THREE: Made a decision to turn our will and our lives over to the care of God as we understood Him.

STEP FOUR: Made a searching and fearless moral inventory of ourselves.

STEP FIVE: Admitted to God, to ourselves, and to another human being the exact nature of our wrongs.

STEP SIX: Were entirely ready to have God remove all these defects of character.

STEP SEVEN: Humbly asked Him to remove our shortcomings.

STEP EIGHT: Made a list of all persons we had harmed, and became willing to make amends to them all.

STEP NINE: Made direct amends to such people wherever possible, except when to do so would injure them or others.

STEP TEN: Continued to take personal inventory and when we were wrong promptly admitted it.

STEP ELEVEN: Sought through prayer and meditation to improve our conscious contact with God, as we understood Him, praying only for knowledge of His will for us and the power to carry that out.

STEP TWELVE: Having had a spiritual awakening as the result of these steps, we tried to carry this message to alcoholics, and to practice these principles in all our affairs.

The Twelve Steps & Related Scripture

STEP ONE

We admitted we were powerless over the effects of our separation from God—that our lives had become unmanageable.

I know nothing good lives in me, that is, in my sinful nature. For I have the desire to do what is good, but I cannot carry it out. (Romans 7:18)

STEP TWO

Came to believe that a power greater than ourselves could restore us to sanity.

For it is God who works in you to will and to act according to his good purpose (Philippians 2:13)

STEP THREE

Made a decision to turn our will and our lives over to the care of God as we understood Him.

Therefore, I urge you, brothers, in view of God's mercy, to offer your bodies as living sacrifices, holy and pleasing to God—which is your spiritual worship. (Romans 12:1)

STEP FOUR

Made a searching and fearless moral inventory of ourselves.

Let us examine our ways and test them, and let us return to the Lord. (Lamentations 3:40)

STEP FIVE

Admitted to God, to ourselves, and to another human being the exact nature of our wrongs.

Therefore confess your sins to each other and pray for each other so that you may be healed. *(James 5–16a)*

STEP SIX

Were entirely ready to have God remove all these defects of character.

Humble yourselves before the Lord, and he will lift you up. *(James 4:10)*

STEP SEVEN

Humbly asked Him to remove our shortcomings.

If we confess our sins, he is faithful and just and will forgive us our sins and purify us from all unrighteousness. *(1 John 1:9)*

STEP EIGHT

Made a list of all persons we had harmed, and became willing to make amends to them all.

Do unto others as you would have them do to you. *(Luke 6:31)*

STEP NINE

Made direct amends to such people wherever possible, except when to do so would injure them or others.

Therefore, if you are offering your gift at the altar and there remember that your brother has something against you, leave your gift there in front of the altar. First go and be reconciled to your brother; then come and offer your gift. *(Matthew 5:23–24)*

STEP TEN

Continued to take personal inventory and when we were wrong promptly admitted it.

So, if you think you are standing firm, be careful that you don't fall. *(1 Corinthians 10:12)*

STEP ELEVEN

Sought through prayer and meditation to improve our conscious contact with God, as we understood Him, praying only for knowledge of His will for us and the power to carry that out.

Let the word of Christ dwell in you richly.
(Colossians 3:16a)

STEP TWELVE

Having had a spiritual awakening as the result of these steps, we tried to carry this message to others, and to practice these principles in all our affairs.

Brothers, if someone is caught in a sin, you who are spiritual should restore him gently. But watch yourself, or you also may be tempted. (Galatians 6:1)

Prayers for

The Twelve Steps—
A Spiritual Journey

Introduction to Prayer

"Lord, teach us to pray." Those were the words of Jesus' disciples as they asked their master for a lesson in prayer. Remember that Jesus' disciples were not skilled theologians or temple priests. They were ordinary men who came from ordinary walks of life: fishers, common laborers, farmers, and even one tax gatherer named Matthew.

Like many of us who are in recovery, the disciples found the idea of praying as Jesus did somewhat foreign and even uncomfortable. They had, of course, heard prayers in their local synagogues and maybe in the temple itself. They knew prayers, but they didn't know how to pray. They had never learned to pray the way Jesus prayed.

PRAYER AND CHRIST

Jesus often spent extended times and seasons in solitary prayer. The disciples undoubtedly wondered what he could possibly be praying about for so long, but Jesus wasn't reciting rote petitions. He has fellowshipping with his heavenly Father through conversational prayer. Jesus demonstrated through example that prayer was more than rigid recitation—it was caring communication and familial fellowship with God.

Jesus was a man of prayer. He prayed and fasted for forty days before he began his ministry. He prayed all night the day before he chose his twelve disciples. He spent long hours in meditative prayer to recharge his spirit after exhausting ministry among the masses.

Looking into the future, to a time when he would no longer be with them, Jesus asked his Father to look out for his disciples and all Christians in the ages to come. The seventeenth chapter of the Gospel of John recounts his prayer. Jesus is asking his Father to make sure things are OK after he, Jesus, is no longer with his disciples. He wants to make sure that his Father will make himself known to them and will protect them.

Before his passion and crucifixion, Jesus prayed in the Garden of Gethsemane as he struggled with and finally surrendered to his Father's will. And on the cross of Golgotha, Jesus prayed. While in torment and agony, Jesus prayed for his executioners, and he prayed for himself. In the life of Jesus, we see virtually every type of prayer, from petition to praise.

If we are honest with ourselves, we too need to ask the Lord, "Teach us to pray."

KINDS OF PRAYER

Unfortunately, prayer today is often limited to petitions. Petitions are those prayers that ask for something. But prayer is not that narrow. Praying to God is no different from communicating with any other person. Yes, God is a person. And we are his children created in his image for fellowship with him. In prayer, we can—and should—talk with God as we might talk with our spouses, parents, children, friends, and colleagues. We can tell God about anything and everything in our lives—the good, the bad, the failures, successes, even things we can't talk about with another human being. God wants us to ask for things, but he also wants to lament with us and rejoice with us. He wants to hear about our concerns for others and our problems with them. He wants to hear what we're thankful for.

This book is more than just an aid for Step Eleven, in which we seek "through prayer and meditation to improve our conscious contact with God." Its intent is to help the reader develop a lifestyle of prayer and a daily habit of communication with his or her Higher Power. In this book of prayers, we focus on ten biblical categories or types of prayer: petition, declaration, complaint, meditation, submission, penitence, imprecation, intercession, thanksgiving, and praise.

PRAYER AND THIS BOOK

The opening chapter explores prayers for each of the Twelve Steps. In the following chapters, the ten categories of prayer are discussed in detail, one to a chapter. Each chapter includes examples of that kind of prayer to aid the reader in improving his or her prayer life. You can use these prayers as they are written, or you can use them to help you begin to articulate your own personal concerns, distinctive circumstances, specific gratitude, personalized praise, and individual style of talking directly to God. To that end, there is also a chapter about the practice of prayer.

This book is intended to be a companion to *The Twelve Steps—A Spiritual Journey* (Recovery Publications, Inc.) workbook. It can be used to provide specific prayers for each step study. It can be used as a tool to equip the reader with ideas on how prayer can aid every area of recovery.

And this book can serve as a guide to Christian prayer in general. Our recovery is a spiritual journey, but it is not a journey that we need travel alone. Prayer helps us keep in contact with our greatest guide, our sufficient supplier, and our constant companion—prayer keeps us in contact with our God.

Chapter One

Prayers for the Twelve Steps

To help us keep our program
God-centered.

*Since, then, you have been raised with Christ,
set your hearts on things above, where Christ is
seated at the right hand of God.*
                                            —Col. 3:1 NIV

The Twelve-Step program is divine powered, not human powered. God is the source of our power and our progress. Therefore, daily contact with him is all important. And we make that contact with him out of spiritual desire, not out of religious compulsion. It has been said that religious people are those who work very hard to please God in order to stay out of hell, and spiritual people are those who really want to know God better because they have already been there. We who are in recovery are on the way back from hell. We aren't trying to placate an angry God or to accumulate brownie points. We are hungry to learn God's way and his plan because our way of life and our plan of survival didn't work. Prayer helps us find God's way and plan.

Twelve-Step prayers are different from the kind of prayers most of us have been used to. We understand in Twelve-Step programs that prayer isn't a self-indulgent petition for favors, and we learn that God cannot be manipulated by our pleading. We replace demanding prayers and wish lists with prayers of submission, penitence, and petition for knowledge of God's will.

The Twelve Steps direct us explicitly, and implicitly, to pray and to maintain our connection with God, our Higher Power. The Apostle Paul tells us in the New Testament to "pray without ceasing," and that admonition is especially appropriate for the Twelve-Step program. As believers and as participants in the program, it is our goal to season our lives and our recovery with continual prayer. As believers, we covet God's participation in our recovery, and we use prayer as an invitation for God's involvement.

***STEP ONE:** We admitted we were powerless over the effects of our separation from God—that our lives had become unmanageable.*

The Twelve Steps begin with our acknowledgment of powerlessness. We learn through the pain and unmanageability of our lives that we cannot control our lives or the lives of others. Under our own management, our lives have failed, not prospered. In Step One, all we need to do is admit this understanding. Therefore, Step One implicitly calls for a prayer of admission or surrender. In biblical terms, it is also a complaint, a cry for help from someone caught in an unmanageable situation.

In Step One we might cry out, "Help! I quit! I can't manage life on my own. Life stinks, and I don't know how to change." This "prayer" may or may not be directed at God. It is an honest cry of pain and a genuine call for help. God hears.

FIRST STEP PRAYER

Today, I ask for help with my addiction. Denial has kept me from seeing how powerless I am and how my life is unmanageable. I need to learn and remember that I have an incurable illness and that abstinence is the only way to deal with it.

TO BE HONEST, GOD

To be honest, I'm not sure who I'm praying to.
Maybe I'm talking to myself, but...

To be honest, I can't take any more.
My life is a failure, I feel like a...

To be honest, I want to die, I want to quit.
I want to quit hurting me, I want to quit hurting them.
To be honest, I don't know what to do.
For the first time, I'm really lost...
To be honest, I don't know if anyone hears me.
But if someone hears, please come find me.

LET GO, LET GOD

Higher Power, help me to understand:

To "let go" does not mean to stop caring; it means I can't do it for someone else.

To "let go" is not to enable but to allow learning from natural consequences.

To "let go" is to admit powerlessness, which means the outcome is not in my hands.

To "let go" is not to try to change or blame another, it's to make the most of myself.

To "let go" is not to care for but to care about.

To "let go" is not to fix but to be supportive.

To "let go" is not to judge but to allow another to be a human being.

To "let go" is not to protect, it's to permit another to face reality.

To "let go" is not to deny but to accept.

To "let go" is not to nag, scold, or argue but instead to search out my own shortcomings and correct them.

To "let go" is not to adjust everything to my desires but to take each day as it comes and cherish myself in it.

STEP TWO: *Came to believe that a power greater than ourselves could restore us to sanity.*

After Step One, we are left rather empty and wanting. That's where God comes in. In Step Two, we begin to exercise faith—faith that God provides. We simply believe that a power greater than ourselves can restore us to sanity and take care of us. We are not required to put a name on God in Step Two. We simply exercise a bud of faith that God is causing to grow in our hearts.

A Step Two prayer is implicitly an immature prayer of trust. We might pray, "Somehow I know that you can hear me God—don't ask me how. I also know that you can help me find my way back."

SECOND STEP PRAYER

I pray for an open mind so I may come to believe in a power greater than myself. I pray for humility and the continued opportunity to increase my faith. I don't want to be crazy any more.

GREATER THAN MYSELF

Higher Power,
The sky over my head,
The generations that come before,
The stars that shine above,
The world and its creatures,
The body in which I live,
The sun that warms,
The air I breathe,
The order and way of the universe,
All these things are greater than I am.
Who am I to doubt you God?

A BEGINNER'S PRAYER

Lord, I want to love you,
yet I am not sure.
I want to trust you,
yet I am afraid of being taken in.

I know I need you,
but I am ashamed of the need.
I want to pray,
but I am afraid of being a hypocrite.
I need my independence,
yet I fear to be alone.
I want to belong,
yet I must be myself.
Take me, Lord,
yet leave me alone.
Lord, I believe;
help thou my unbelief.
O Lord, if you are there,
you do understand, don't you?
Give me what I need,
but leave me free to choose.
Help me work it out my own way,
but don't let me go.
Let me understand myself,
but don't let me despair.
Come unto me, O Lord, I want you there.
Lighten my darkness,
but don't dazzle me.
Help me to see what I need to do,
and give me strength to do it.
O Lord, I believe;
help thou my unbelief.

STEP THREE: *Made a decision to turn our will and our lives over to the care of God as we understood Him.*

In Step Three, we come to a place of decision, not action. We decide to turn our will and our lives over to the care of God as we are growing to understand him. This decision, by itself, creates a new serenity in our lives, and it prepares us for the introspective action of Step Four.

Step Three invites us to prayerfully declare an attitude of submission to and confidence in God's will and control. We might pray, "God, part of me knows that you can handle my life better than I can. Although it frightens me, I think I've decided to give you control of my life."

THIRD STEP PRAYER

God,
I offer myself to thee, to build with me and to do with me as thou wilt. Relieve me of the bondage of self, that I may better do thy will. Take away my difficulties, that victory over them may bear witness to those I would help of thy power, thy love, and thy way of life. May I do thy will always!

I CAN MAKE A DECISION

Lord,
I am learning that there is an awful lot I can't do.
I can't control life the way I am used to.
I can't make people be what I want.
I can't stop the pain inside me.
I can't even fully submit to your plan yet—I'm still too frightened
   of you.
But I know that there is one thing I can do right now.
I can make a decision to turn my will and my life over to you.
Making the decision doesn't mean I have to make it happen.
Making the decision doesn't mean I understand you or your pla
Making the decision doesn't even mean I'm entirely willing, but it
   does mean that I know your way and will is right.
Lord, turn my simple decision into reality.

MY FIRST PRAYER

I surrender to you my entire life,
   O God of my understanding.
I have made a mess of it
   trying to run it myself.
You take it, the whole thing,
   and run it for me,
According to your will and plan.

STEP FOUR: *Made a searching and fearless moral inventory of ourselves.*

In this step, God helps us search our hearts and lives for those defects, shortcomings, and failures that have marked our lives up until this time. This inventory includes more than our failures and sins. It lists our survival techniques—our dysfunctional attempts at living. Step Four also provides for a positive inventory. We are asked to include our positive traits, which is often more difficult than listing our faults. God can transform and use our strength.

Step Four begins a penitent mood of prayer as we search our hearts in moral inventory. The penitent prayers of Step Four begin by asking God to search our hearts. We might pray, "God, you know my faults and shortcomings better than I do. Show me what you see."

FOURTH STEP PRAYER

Dear God,
It is I who have made my life a mess. I have done it, but I cannot undo it. My mistakes are mine, and I will begin a searching and fearless moral inventory. I will write down my wrongs, but I will also include that which is good. I pray for the strength to complete the task.

LIGHT A CANDLE

O God of my understanding,
light a candle within my heart,
that I may see what is therein
and remove the wreckage of the past.

I NEED TO TAKE A TRIP

God, I'm told I need to take a trip—a trip inside myself.
I guess this trip could be pretty hard and very dark.
So I want you to come along and bring your light.
I'm not sure what I'll find; maybe I'll find myself.
I know I'm rough and demanding and always right.
But I'm not sure I'm as rotten as they say.
Maybe I am.

Maybe there's good in there too; do you think so?
Well, I'd better start.
You're coming aren't you, God?
I don't want to go in there alone.

STEP FIVE: *Admitted to God, to ourselves, and to another human being the exact nature of our wrongs.*

Step Five requires confession. We admit to God, to ourselves, and to another human being the exact nature of the wrongs we listed in Step Four. God aids us in this vulnerable process, and if we ask for his help, he directs us to the right "human being" to whom we can admit our wrongs.

Step Five explicitly calls for a penitent prayer as the exact nature of our wrongs is admitted to God. We confess what God revealed to us in Step Four. We might pray, "God, give me the honesty and courage to admit what you showed me about myself. You showed me..."

FIFTH STEP PRAYER

Higher Power,

My inventory has shown me who I am, yet I ask for your help in admitting my wrongs to another person and to you. Assure me, and be with me in this step, for without this step I cannot progress in my recovery. With your help, I can do this, and I will do it.

SHOW ME WHO

Show me who can hear my confession and not hurt me.
Show me who can stand my story and not condemn.
Show me who can listen and honestly care.
Show me who can be a human being and still show mercy.
Show me who can bear to mind my list, which is long.
Show me who can hear the exact nature of my wrongs.

GIVE ME COURAGE

God,

I've never had to tell somebody else about my wrongs.
I've never confessed to a priest or even to my dog.
I've kept it all inside and sought to hide.

I've been too frightened to admit what I really am.
Give me courage to tell somebody else what I've found.

STEP SIX: *Were entirely ready to have God remove all these defects of character.*

Being entirely ready is a state of mind and heart; it's a place at which we must arrive for our recovery to continue. Step Six acknowledges this. The earlier steps, especially Steps Four and Five, have made us acutely aware of our need to change. And now Step Six gives us the time and opportunity to become ready to move on to the work of change that still lies ahead.

Step Six is a change of heart and mind and prepares us for repentance. It implicitly acknowledges the presence and work of God in our lives as he makes us willing to release or repent of our defects. Meditation or "listening prayer" is used in Step Six. We should be cautious not to use many words in Step Six prayers. Instead, we should release distractions and open ourselves to hear God, and we should quiet ourselves to allow God to work.

A Step Six prayer can be a cry for God to quiet our hearts. "Quiet my heart, God, from all the activity and noise. Help me center my thoughts and my mind. Remove the distractions that keep me spinning. I truly desire change; quiet my heart, and make me ready."

SIXTH STEP PRAYER

Dear God,
I am ready for your help in removing from me the defects of character that I now realize are an obstacle to my recovery. Help me to continue being honest with myself and guide me toward spiritual and mental health.

NOW

Dear God,
I don't like what I was.
But I'm not sure what I am.
I was a liar.
Now I'm numb.

I was a manipulator.
    Now I'm frightened of others.
I was a controller.
    Now I'm powerless.
I was a bully.
    Now I'm my own victim.
I was afraid of pain.
    Now I hold pain's hand.
I used to hide in isolation.
    Now I'm locked up with you.
I used to be bold and loud.
    Now I'm afraid to speak.
I used to think only of myself.
    Now I think only about the pain I caused.
I used to trust only in myself.
    Now I am in your hands.
O God, I'm ready, please change me.

QUIET MY HEART

Quiet my heart, God,
    from all the activity and noise.
Help me center my thoughts, my mind.
Remove the distractions that spin me.
My wrongs, my faults lie before you.
You know me inside out—the good, the bad.
Help me receive your inner working and change.
I want to turn my back on yesterday's ways.
I want to truly desire change, lasting change.
So quiet my heart, make me ready.

STEP SEVEN: *Humbly asked Him to remove our shortcomings.*

Humility is also a state of mind and heart. But more, it is the spirit and attitude that controls the rest of our spiritual journey, a journey that humbly relies upon God and that humbly faces those we've damaged and offended. In Step Seven, we come to God not to confess, but to ask. We tried to change, we were determined to do better, but we failed. Now it is time to ask, to humbly ask God to remove what we cannot remove: our sins and our shortcomings.

Step Seven is an explicit call for penitent prayer as we humbly ask God to remove our shortcomings. We might pray, "God, please forgive me, have mercy on me. I see my shortcomings, I see my powerlessness over my faults. I have truly had a change of heart and mind as far as my old ways are concerned. I want you to take them away, please."

SEVENTH STEP PRAYER

My Creator,
I am willing that you should have all of me, good and bad. I pray that you now remove from me every single defect of character which stands in the way of my usefulness to you and my fellows. Grant me strength as I go out from here to do your bidding.

REMOVE THESE

God,
Many times I have tried to change myself.
I have read books, listened to tapes, heard speakers, gone on retreats, taken classes; yet I've always failed.
I have determined to do better, scolded and shamed myself, made New Year's resolutions, exercised self-control; yet I've always failed.
I have tried everything to change, and so now I come to you. I'm sorry that you are my last resort instead of my first hope.
I cannot boast of accomplishment, I cannot show my growth, I bring you only shortcomings and needs. Please, do what I cannot do—remove these.

WHO, ME?

I need to be forgiven, Lord,
    so many times a day.
So often do I stumble and fall.
Be merciful, I pray.
Help me not be critical
    when others' faults I see.
For so often, Lord,
    the same faults are in me.

STEP EIGHT: *Made a list of all persons we had harmed, and became willing to make amends to them all.*

Step Eight provides a time for reflection. Like Step Six, it is a time to become willing to move forward. Unlike Step Six, Step Eight calls for action and asks us to make a list of the persons we have harmed. As the names and faces of friends, family, enemies, associates, and others come before us, we must be ever vigilant to remember that the program is about us, not them. Many of the people whom we will recall and put on our list have hurt and damaged us, too. But we are working our program, not theirs. If we ask, God helps us to see these people from his perspective, not ours.

Step Eight is a time for acknowledging the presence and work of God in our lives as he assists us in the recollection to those whom we have harmed. "Listening prayer" is again called for as we allow God to bring to mind the names and faces of those we have harmed. Once we pray for God's help in making our list, we need to listen.

A prayer for Step Eight might say, "O God, I know I have harmed others along the way. Help me recall the names and faces of those to whom you would have me make amends. Quiet my heart, and center my thoughts on hearing your voice. Keep me from recalling the pain others have caused me. Help me take responsibility."

EIGHTH STEP PRAYER

Higher Power,
 I ask your help in making my list of all those I have harmed.
I will take responsibility for my mistakes, and be forgiving to others as you are forgiving to me. Grant me the willingness to begin my restitution. This I pray.

OPEN MIND

Higher Power, may I understand:
To be alert to my own needs, not to the faults of others;
To remain teachable;
To listen;
To keep an open mind; and
To learn not who's right but what's right.

IT'S ABOUT ME

Help me remember, God, that this program is about me. I find
  myself wanting to judge and blame and accuse everyone but
  myself. I'm supposed to be making a list of all those I have
  harmed, yet my mind is full of those who have offended me. Is
  this some sort of mental defense mechanism to keep myself from
  facing the pain I've caused others?
Help me get over this stumbling block. I release those who hurt
  me. I forgive. I put those people in your hands, God.
Vengeance is yours. Wait, God...don't punish them. I'm just as guilty
  ...don't punish me.
Help me make things right.

STEP NINE: *Made direct amends to such people wherever possible, except when to do so would injure them or others.*

Step Nine, first and foremost, is for us. It is an action step that requires courage and commitment. Step Nine is one of the most powerful steps, and for many it is a very difficult step. When making amends in Step Nine, we make a significant and lasting break from our past behavior and separate ourselves from the mistakes of our past.

Step Nine calls for a prayer of declaration and complaint as we tell God of our fears. God, in return, will nurture the willingness to make the amends that Step Nine calls for. Prayers of petition for courage are helpful as well, as we set out to make amends. We might pray, "God, I'm scared to face some of these people to whom I am to make amends. In fact, God, I spent a great deal of effort avoiding most of the people on my list. Give me courage to face them and this step. Let this step help me put the past behind me."

NINTH STEP PRAYER

Higher Prayer,
    I pray for the right attitude to make my amends, being ever mindful not to harm others in the process. I ask for your guidance in making indirect amends. Most important, I will continue to make amends by staying abstinent, helping others, and growing in spiritual progress.

FINISH THE BUSINESS

Dear God,
Step Nine is a way for me to finish the business that has been left
    undone for so long. For many years I have taken no thought for
    the damage I was doing through my abuse.
I have stolen that which was not mine.
I have broken promises that were meant to last a lifetime.
I have wounded spirits that may never be healed.
I have lost the trust of precious friends and family.
I have used others for my own purpose.
I have lost precious years with loved ones.
I know that you have forgiven me, Higher Power. You accept me.

Now help me reach out in sincerity to make amends. I cannot change the past. I cannot relive the wasted years. But with your help I can say I'm sorry, I can show I've changed and I can finish the business.

EXCUSES

God,

Help me stop making excuses and start making amends. You've heard me say:

I needn't look for this one because he's probably dead.

I don't have to make amends to them, they hurt me more.

I won't call this guy, he wouldn't remember.

I can't talk to him, he'll explode.

I will never reach out to her, she's a gossip.

I can't bear the pain of seeing this one...

No, it won't work...I can't...this is too hard.

Have you heard me make the excuses, God? I used to think I had guts. I used to think I had courage—I don't. Please, God, give me yours.

Help me stop making excuses and start making amends.

STEP TEN: *Continued to take personal inventory and, when we were wrong, promptly admitted it.*

Step Ten is the first of the maintenance steps. This step begins to teach us a way of life that keeps us from falling back into past mistakes and old habit patterns. Step Ten encourages us to examine ourselves daily and make prompt confessions and amends where necessary. The prompt recognition, admission, and correction of our wrongs ensures a lifestyle that fosters recovery and health, day by day.

Step Ten renews the penitent prayer as we seek God's help in searching our lives and seeking his help and forgiveness in daily restitution. We might pray, "God, help me see my life and actions today through your eyes; show me where I have fallen short. Show me your mercy and give me the courage to make things right."

TENTH STEP PRAYER

I pray I may continue:
To grow in understanding and effectiveness;
To take daily spot check inventories of myself;
To correct mistakes when I make them;
To take responsibility for my actions;
To be ever aware of my negative and self-defeating
    attitudes and behaviors;
To keep my willfulness in check;
To always remember I need your help;
To keep love and tolerance of others as my code; and
To consider in daily prayer how I can best serve you,
    my Higher Power.

"TO BE" PRAYER

O Lord, I ain't what I ought to be,
and I ain't what I want to be,
and I ain't what I'm going to be.
But O Lord, I thank you
that I ain't what I used to be.

FIRST THINGS FIRST

Dear Higher Power, remind me:
To tidy up my own mind;
To keep any sense of values straight;
To sort out the possible and the impossible;
To turn the impossible over to you; and
Get busy on the possible.

TO CHANGE

I pray that I may continue to change, and
I appreciate you for investing in me your time, your patience,
    your understanding, and for seeing in me someone worthwhile.
I am sorry for the past—but I will change for the better, and
    I am grateful for the opportunity!

STEP ELEVEN: *Sought through prayer and meditation to improve our conscious contact with God as we understood Him, praying only for knowledge of His will for us and the power to carry that out.*

Step eleven is the maintenance step that keeps us in touch with God. Through daily prayer and meditation, we develop a God-consciousness that helps our daily living. Prayer is a time to connect with God, an opportunity to ask for direction. God already has a wonderful plan for our lives. It is our job to ask him what that plan is and to ask him for the strength to accomplish it.

Step Eleven explicitly calls for the sort of prayerful petition and spiritual meditation that draws us into daily fellowship with God. We might pray, "God, show me what your will is for me today. I admit that doing your will and not mine is sometimes scary. I pray that you will also give me the courage and ability to carry out your plan, not mine."

ELEVENTH STEP PRAYER

Higher Power, as I understand you,
  I pray to keep my connection with you open and clear from the confusion of daily life. Through my prayers and meditations, I ask especially for freedom from self-will, relationalization, and wishful thinking. I pray for the guidance of correct thought and positive action. Your will, Higher Power, not mine, be done.

HELP ME KNOW HOW

God,
  I don't always know how to pray, and when I do pray, I'm not sure that you really hear me. I know you do, but I wish that you would help me feel your closeness, sense your warmth, and know your acceptance and love as I come to you in prayer. When I meditate on your messages to me from scripture, from others, or from your handiwork in nature, draw near to me. And whether you draw near to me in meditation or whether I come to you in prayer, help me to always depart our times together with a greater understanding of your will for my life. I want to please—help me know how.

LANGUAGE OF THE HEART

Dear God,
You know my needs before I ask,
  my heart before I pray, and
  my gratitude before I even offer my thanks.
You understand me better than I understand myself,
  and I thank you for communicating with me in the language
  of the heart.

STEP TWELVE: *Having had a spiritual awakening as the result of these Steps, we tried to carry this message to others, and to practice these principles in all our affairs.*

Step Twelve acknowledges openly that the Twelve-Step program is, indeed, a spiritual journey. Accepting the steps as a way of life can result in a spiritual awakening as we are directed to the basic principles of the kingdom of God. There is an important mission in Step Twelve—that we share this spiritual program with others and demonstrate its principles in our daily affairs.

Step Twelve implicitly calls for petitions that invoke courage and commitment as the program is shared with others and practiced daily in our lives. We might pray, "God, show me how I can best share the program with others. Help me not to judge. Keep me ever mindful that this program is a way of life and that I need to practice it in my everyday living."

TWELFTH STEP PRAYER

Dear God,
My spiritual awakening continues to unfold. The help I have received I shall pass on and give to others, both in and out of the fellowship. For this opportunity I am grateful.

I pray most humbly to continue walking day by day on the road of spiritual progress. I pray for the inner strength and wisdom to practice the principles of this way of life in all I do and say. I need you, my friends, and the program every hour of every day.

This is a better way to live.

THANK YOU, GOD

Thank you, God, for all you have given me.
Thank you for all you have taken from me.
But, most of all, I thank you, God, for what you've left me:
recovery, along with peace of mind, faith, hope, and love.

THE TWELVE STEPS PRAYER

Power, greater than myself, as I understand you,
I willingly admit that without your help, I am powerless over
  my dependencies and my life has become unmanageable.
I believe you can restore me to sanity.
I turn my life and my will over to you.
I have made a searching and fearless moral inventory of myself.
I admit to you, to myself, and to another the exact nature of my
  wrongs.
I am entirely ready to have you remove these defects of character.
I humbly ask you to remove my shortcomings.
I have made direct amends to all persons I have harmed, except
  when to do so would injure them or others.
I will continue to take personal inventory, and when I am wrong,
  I will promptly admit it.
I seek through prayer and meditation to improve my conscious
  contact with you and pray only for knowledge of your will
  for me and the power to carry it out.
I ask for the grace to carry the message of your help unto others and
  to practice the principles of the Twelve Steps in all my affairs.

Meeting Prayers

MEETING PRAYER NO. 1

Our Father, we come to you as a friend.

You have said that, where two or three are gathered in your name, there you will be in the midst. We believe you are with us now.

We believe this is something you would have us do, and that it has your blessing.

We believe that you want us to be real partners with you in this business of living, accepting our full responsibility and certain that the rewards will be freedom, growth, and happiness.

For this, we are grateful.

We ask you, at all times, to guide us.

Help us daily to come closer to you, and grant us new ways of living our gratitude.

MEETING PRAYER NO. 2

Our Heavenly Father,

We ask your blessings on this meeting. Please bless the spirit and the purpose of this group.

Give us strength to follow this program according to your will and in all humility.

Forgive us for yesterday, and grant us courage for today and hope for tomorrow.

MEETING PRAYER NO. 3

God bless this meeting and the members gathered here tonight.

Help us to make this group a haven of strength and comfort, giving to all who seek help here the beauty and friendliness of home, which shall be as a shield against temptation of all kinds and against loneliness and despair.

Bless those who are going forth from this house to fight the gallant fight, to know suffering; and bless those who come here to rest, those who must readjust themselves to face life once more.

Chapter Two

Prayers of Petition

For knowledge of God's will for us
and for the power and other resources
to carry that out.

*This is the confidence we have in approaching
God: that if we ask anything according to his
will, he hears us. And if we know that he hears
us—whatever we ask—we know that we have
what we asked of him. —1 John 5:14–15 NIV*

*P*rayers of petition are the most commonly prayed prayers. When we want something of God, we petition him. Prayers of petition are requests to God for help in times of need, health in times of illness, provision in times of want, special favors in times of longing, and safety in times of danger. The times and circumstances for petitioning God's help, provision, and grace are endless. We humans are a needy lot, and once we have broken through our denial and fully embraced Step One, we understand our need. And we can feel comfortable going to God as children approaching a loving father.

Prayers asking for clarity to realize and follow God's will are also prayers of petition. The Twelve-Step program continually encourages us to place this particular petition above all others; we are counseled to pray for God's will. The wisdom of the Twelve Steps is most evident in this as it emphasizes the important issue of control, or rather our lack of it.

The authors of the Twelve Steps pointed out long ago, in the *Big Book of Alcoholics Anonymous*, that our problems are not rooted in one particular compulsion, addiction, or drug of choice. They are rooted in the issue of who is in control of our lives. By the time we grasp the direction and aim of the Twelve Steps, we understand that God, our Higher Power, is in control because we have surrendered our lives to his care. And that surrender becomes our greatest source of serenity.

Step One helps us admit our powerlessness. Step Two opens our eyes to a power greater than ourselves. Step Three brings us to a place of decision as we turn our will and our lives over to God. Steps Four through Ten help us see our failures and defects and humbly seek

God's help in our deliverance and continual cleansing. So, as we learn dependence on God and learn to entrust our life and recovery to him, why would we want to petition God for what *we think* is best for us?

The most appropriate petition we can pray is to discern God's will for our lives and be given the power to carry out his will. But what about all our needs? The Bible makes it clear that God knows our needs and that it is his will that those needs be met. Remember Jesus' admonition:

> "So do not worry, saying, 'What shall we eat?' or 'What shall we drink?' or 'What shall we wear?' For the pagans [those who do not know our loving and gracious God] run after all these things, and your heavenly Father knows that you need them. But seek first his kingdom [his rulership and right to reign in your life] and his righteousness, and all these things will be given to you as well." (Matt. 6:31–33 NIV)

God's will is still best, and always will be. Our will and our control only brought us sorrow, pain, and mismanagement. His will brings life, peace, and order. Hear the word of God for us: "'For I know the plans I have for you,' declares the Lord, 'plans to prosper you and not to harm you, plans to give you hope and a future.'" (Jer. 29:11 NIV)

Can we make petitions for things other than knowledge of God's will? Of course, but when we know what God's will is for our lives, we can pray other petitions with great confidence. In John's first epistle we find these words:

> This is the confidence we have in approaching God: that if we ask anything according to his will, he hears us. And if we know that he hears us—whatever we ask—we know that we have what we asked of him. (1 John 5:14–15 NIV)

On the other hand, James describes the outcome of petitions that are self-willed and self-indulgent: "You ask and do not receive, because you ask amiss, that you may spend it on your pleasures [lusts]." (James 4:3 NIV)

Prayers of Petition for God's Will

The most appropriate petition we can pray is a petition to discern God's will for our lives and for the power to carry out his will. So we begin with prayers for God's will. The following are prayers of petition for knowledge of God's will for us and the power to carry out his will. These prayers can be used as guides for developing our own prayers for God's will.

PEACE IN GOD'S WILL

My Higher Power, quicken my spirit and fix my thoughts on your will, that I may see what you would have done and contemplate its doing without self-consciousness or inner excitement, without haste and without delay, without fear of other people's judgments, and without anxiety about success. Knowing only that it is your will and therefore must be done quietly, faithfully, and lovingly, for in your will alone is my peace.

Jesus said to them, "My food is to do the will of him who sent me, and to finish his work." —John 4:34 *NIV*

SERENITY PRAYER

God, grant me the serenity to accept the things I cannot change;
The courage to change the things I can;
The wisdom to know the difference.
Living one day at a time;
Enjoying one moment at a time;
Accepting hardship as the pathway to peace;
Taking, as he did, this sinful world as it is, not as I would

have it;
Trusting that he will make all things right if I surrender to his will;
That I may be reasonably happy in this life, and supremely
 happy with him forever in the next.

You will keep in perfect peace him whose mind is steadfast, because he
trusts in you.   —*Isa. 26:3 NIV*

MY DAILY PRAYER

God,
   I turn my will and my life over to you this day for your keeping.
Your will, Lord, not mine. I ask for your guidance and direction. I
will walk humbly with you and your creations. You are giving me a
grateful heart for my many blessings. You are removing the defects of
character that stand in my way. You are giving me freedom from
self-will.
   Let love, compassion, and understanding be in my every thought,
word, and deed this day. I release those to you who have mistreated
me. I truly desire your abundance of truth, love, harmony, and
peace. As I go out today to do your bidding, let me help anyone I
can who is less fortunate than I.

I will instruct you and teach you in the way you should go; I will
counsel you and watch over you.   —*Ps. 32:8 NIV*

CHANGES

Today I pray that I may understand there are some things I cannot
 change;
I cannot change the weather.
I cannot change the tick of the clock.
I cannot change the past.
I cannot change other people against their will.
I cannot change what is right and wrong.
I cannot change the fact that a relationship ended.
I can stop worrying over that which I cannot change and *enjoy living*
 more! I can place those things into the hands of the *one who is*
 bigger than I. Save energy. Let go. Instead of trying to change
 someone else:

I can change my attitude.

I can change my list of priorities.

I can change my bad habits into good ones.

I can move from the place of brokenness into wholeness, into the
beautiful person *God* created me to become.

*You were taught, with regard to your former way of life, to put off your
old self, which is being corrupted by its deceitful desires; to be made new
in the attitude of your minds; and to put on the new self, created to be
like God in true righteousness and holiness.* —*Eph. 4:22–23* NIV

ON AWAKENING

God, please direct my thinking, to move it away from self-pity,
and from dishonest and self-seeking motives.

As I go through the day and face indecision, please give me inspiration, an intuitive thought, or a decision. Make me relax and take it
easy; don't let me struggle. Let me rely upon *your* inspiration, intuitive thoughts, and decisions instead of my old ideas.

Show me all through the day what my next step is to be, and give
me whatever I need to take care of each problem. God, I ask you
especially for freedom from self-will, and I make no requests for
myself only. But give me the knowledge of your will for me and the
power to carry it out in every contact during the day.

As I go through this day, let me pause when agitated or doubtful
and ask you for the right thought or action. Let me constantly be
reminded that I am no longer running the show. I will humbly say
many times each day, "your will be done" and I will agree that it is.

I will then be in much less danger of excitement, fear, anger,
worry, self-pity, or foolish decisions. I will be more efficient. I won't
be burning up energy foolishly as I was when trying to run life to
suit myself. I will let you discipline me in this simple way. I will give
you all the power and all the praise.

*In the morning, O Lord, you hear my voice; in the morning I lay my
requests before you and wait in expectation.* —*Ps. 5:3* NIV

A MORNING PRAYER

Good morning, God. You are ushering in another day, all nice and
freshly new.
Here I come again, dear Lord. Please renew me, too.
Forgive the many errors that I made yesterday and let me come
again, dear God, to walk in your own way.
But, God, you know I cannot do it on my own.
Please take my hand and hold it tight, for I cannot walk alone.

Yet I am always with you; you hold me by my right hand. You guide me
with your counsel. . . —*Ps. 73:23–24a NIV*

ETERNAL GOD

Eternal God, we know you forgive our trespasses if we forgive
ourselves and others.
We know you protect us from destructive temptation if we continue
to seek your help and guidance.
We know you provide us food and shelter today if we but place our
trust in you and try to do our best.
Give us this day knowledge of your will for us and the power to
carry it out.
For yours is infinite power and love, forever.

I love the Lord, for he heard my voice; he heard my cry for mercy.
—*Ps. 116:1 NIV*

UNSELFISHNESS PRAYER

Higher Power, guide me as I walk the narrow way between being
selfish and unselfish. I know I must be selfish, to concentrate on my
own recovery, so I do not slip and be of no use to myself or anyone
else. Yet I must also be unselfish, reaching out to others, sensitive to
their needs, and willing to meet them at any time. With your help, I
can do both, and keep a balance that will give me a right perspective
in my life.

I guide you in the way of wisdom and lead you along straight paths.
—*Prov. 4:11 NIV*

WHAT IS BEST

O Lord, you know what is best for me.
Let this or that be done, as you please.
Give what you will, how much you will, and when you will.

Yet not my will, but yours be done.   —*Luke 22:42b NIV*

PRAYER TO KNOW

Grant it to me, Higher Power:
To know that which is worth knowing,
To love that which is worth loving,
To praise that which pleases you most,
To work for that which helps others.
Grant it to me:
To distinguish with true judgment things that differ, and above
    all to search out, and to do what is well pleasing to you.

*Finally, brothers, whatever is true, whatever is noble, whatever is right,
whatever is pure, whatever is lovely, whatever is admirable—if anything
is excellent or praiseworthy—think about such things.* —*Phil. 4:8 NIV*

GUIDE ME

Thank you, Higher Power, for this beautiful day, for strength,
    for health.
Help me to live this day for you.
Place in my pathway some way to serve others.
Help me to know that no other walks in my shoes, that there is
    something that only I can do today.
Guide my thoughts and deeds that I may feel your presence today
    and in all the tomorrows.

*You have made known to me the path of life; you will fill me with joy in
your presence, with eternal pleasures at your right hand.*
    —*Ps. 16:11 NIV*

TEACH ME

Teach me, God, so that I might know
    the way to change and the way to grow.
Give me the words to ask you how
    to handle the here and live in the now.
Tempt me not with the valleys of death,
    give me freedom from fear in every breath.
And though mistakes I make in my daily life,
    deliver me from aiding strife.
Understand me God, as I am now,
    and show me the furrows I need to plow
    to reach my goal as a ripening food,
    so I might feed others all that is good.
Fill me with energy known as the power,
    till I come to rest at the midnight hour.

Show me your ways, O Lord, teach me your paths. —Ps. 25:4 NIV

RUN THE RACE

Help me this day, Higher Power, to run with patience the race that is
    set before me.
May neither opposition without nor discouragement within divert
    me from my progress in recovery.
Inspire in me strength of mind, willingness, and acceptance, that I
    may meet all fears and difficulties with courage, and may com-
    plete the tasks set before me today.

*Let your eyes look straight ahead, fix your gaze directly before you. Make
level paths for your feet and take only ways that are firm. Do not swerve
to the right or the left; keep your foot from evil.* —Prov. 4:25–27 NIV

Prayers of Petition

With an understanding of God's will for us (including the affirmations of God's word like Jesus' assurance of basic provisions mentioned earlier), we can pray other petitions with confidence. Let us learn from them and begin to develop our own unique prayers of petition.

THE LORD'S PRAYER

One day Jesus was praying in a certain place. When he had finished, one of his disciples said to him, "Lord, teach us to pray as John taught his disciples."
—*Luke 11:1 NIV*

Our Father, who art in heaven, hallowed by thy name.
Thy kingdom come. Thy will be done, on earth as it is in heaven.
Give us this day our daily bread. And forgive us our trespasses, as we
    forgive those who trespass against us. And lead us not into temp-
    tation, but deliver us from evil. For thine is the kingdom and the
    power and the glory, forever and ever.

PRAYER FOR THE HURRIED

Lord, slow me down.
    Ease the pounding of my heart by quieting my mind. Steady
my hurried pace. Give me, in the confusion of my day, the calmness
of the everlasting hills. Break the tension of my nerves and muscles.
Help me to know the magical, restoring power of sleep.
    Teach me to take minute vacations by slowing down to look at a
flower, a cloud, to chat with a friend, to pat a dog, or to read a few
lines from a good book. Remind me that the race is not always to the
swift, that there is more to life than increasing speed.

Let me look upward into the branches of the towering oak and know that it grew great and strong because it grew slowly and well.

Lord, slow me down. Inspire me to send my roots deep into the soil of life's enduring values that I may grow toward the stars of my great destiny.

In vain you rise early and stay up late, toiling for food to eat—for he grants sleep to those he loves. —Ps. 127:2 NIV

THE TOLERANCE PRAYER

Lord, give me tolerance toward those whose thoughts and ways, in both the program and in life, conflict with mine.

For though I would like to, I cannot always know what constitutes the Absolute Truth. The other person may be right, while I may be all wrong, yet unaware.

Lord, make my motives right, for only this can ease my conscience when I sometimes err.

Lord, give me tolerance, for who am I to stand in judgment on another person's mistakes? No one knows better than my inward self how many little blunders I have made and can make.

Life is full of stones that somehow trip us, and meaning not, we stumble now and then.

Lord, give me tolerance, for only you are rightly fit to judge my fellow travelers.

There is only one Lawgiver and Judge, the one who is able to save and destroy. But you—who are you to judge your neighbor?
                                                            —James 4:12 NIV

THE ACCEPTANCE PRAYER

God, grant me the serenity to accept my addiction gracefully and humbly. Grant me also the ability to absorb the teachings of the program, which by its past experience is trying to help me. Teach me to be grateful for the help I receive.

Guide me, Higher Power, in the path of tolerance and understanding of my fellow members and fellow humans; guide me away from the path of criticism, intolerance, jealousy, and envy of my friends. Let me not prejudge; let me not become a moralist; keep my tongue and thoughts from malicious idle gossip.

Help me to grow in stature spiritually, mentally, and morally.
Grant me that greatest of all rewards, that of being able to help my
fellow sufferers in their search out of the addiction that has encom-
passed them.
Above all, help me to be less critical and impatient with myself.

Instead, speaking the truth in love, we will in all things grow up into
him who is the Head, that is, Christ.   —*Eph. 4:15 NIV*

GOD, HELP ME LIVE TODAY

God, more than anything else in this world, I just don't want to be
   sick any more.
God, grant me the serenity to accept the things I cannot change
   (people, places, and things), the courage to change the things I
   can (my attitudes), and the common sense to know the difference.
God, help me, please, stay clean and sober this day, even if it's in
   spite of myself. Help me, Lord, stay sensitive to my own needs
   and the things that are good for me, the needs of others, and the
   things that are good for them.
And if you please, Lord, free me enough of the bondage of self that I
   may be of some useful value as a human being, whether I understand or not; that I may carry my own keys, maintain my own in-
   tegrity, and live this day at peace with you, at peace with myself,
   and at peace with the world I live in, just for today.
God, help me in this day, demonstrate that:
It is good for me to love and to be loved.
It is good for me to understand and to be understood.
It is good for me to give and to receive.
It is good for me to comfort and to allow myself to be comforted.
And it is obviously far better for me to be useful as a human being
   than it is to be selfish.
God, help me please put one foot in front of the other, keep moving
   forward, and do the best I can with what I have to work with to-
   day, accepting the results of whatever that may or may not be.

"In the time of my favor I heard you, and in the day of salvation I
helped you." I tell you, now is the time of God's favor, now is the day
of salvation.   —*2 Cor. 6:2 NIV*

ENOUGH TO NEED

Dear God, never allow me to think that I have knowledge enough to need no teaching, wisdom enough to need no correction, talents enough to need no grace, goodness enough to need no progress, humility enough to need no repentance, devotion enough to need no improvement, strength sufficient without your spirit—lest, standing still, I fall back forevermore.

Therefore let him who thinks he stands take heed lest he fall.
—1 Cor. 10:12 NKJV

THE GIFTS I ASK

These are the gifts I ask,
Spirit serene:
Strength for the daily task,
Courage to face the road,
Good cheer to help me
Bear the traveler's load;
And for the hours that come between,
An inward joy in all things heard and seen.

But my eyes are fixed on you, O Sovereign Lord; in you I take refuge...
—Ps. 141:8 NIV

TAKE TIME

Today I pray that I can:
Take time to think.
    It is the source of power.
Take time to play.
    It is the secret of perpetual youth.
Take time to read.
    It is the fountain of wisdom.
Take time to pray.
    It is the greatest power on earth.
Take time to be friendly.
    It is the road to happiness.
Take time to laugh.
    It is the music of the soul.
Take time to give.
    It is too short a day to be selfish.
Take time to work.
    It is the price of success.
Take time to do charity.
    It is the key to heaven.

To everything there is a season,
A time for every purpose under heaven:
A time to be born,
And a time to die;
A time to plant,
And a time to pluck what is planted;
A time to kill,
And a time to heal;
A time to break down,
And a time to build up;
A time to weep,
And a time to laugh;
A time to mourn,
And a time to dance;
A time to cast away stones,
And a time to gather stones;
A time to embrace,
And a time to refrain from embracing;
A time to gain,

And a time to lose;
A time to keep,
And a time to throw away;
A time to tear,
And a time to sew;
A time to keep silence,
And a time to speak;
A time to love,
And a time to hate;
A time of war,
And a time of peace.   —*Eccles. 3:1–8 NKJV*

GOD OF TIME

God of time, God of me,
Even as the earth has times and seasons for the business of life, help
me understand the times and seasons of my life.

Why, do you not even know what will happen tomorrow. What is your
life? You are a mist that appears for a little while and then vanishes.
                                        —*James 4:14 NIV*

RELIANCE ON GOD

O Higher Power,
Never let me think
that I can stand by myself,
and not need you.

"I am the vine; you are the branches. If a man remains in me and I in
him, he will bear much fruit; apart from me you can do nothing."
                                        —*John 15:5 NIV*

SAILOR'S PRAYER

Dear God, be good to me.
The sea is so wide, and my boat is so small.

Where can I go from your Spirit? Where can I flee from your presence?
If I go up to the heavens, you are there; if I make my bed in the depths,
you are there. If I rise on the wings of the dawn, if I settle on the far

side of the sea, even there your hand will guide me, your right hand will
hold me fast.   —*Ps. 139:7–10* NIV

HELP ME REMEMBER

Lord,
Help me remember that nothing is going to happen to me today that
   you and I together can't handle.

Even though I walk through the valley of the shadow of death, I will
fear no evil, for you are with me.   —*Ps. 23:4* NIV

PLEASE, LORD

Please, Lord,
Teach us to laugh again; but God, don't ever let us forget that
we cried.

Weeping may endure for a night, but joy comes in the morning.
                                                          —*Ps. 30:5b* NIV

LIFE IS A CELEBRATION

Lord, help me today to:
Mend a quarrel.
Seek out a forgotten friend.
Dismiss suspicion and replace it with trust.
Write a friendly letter.
Share a treasure.

Give a soft answer.
Encourage another.
Manifest my loyalty in word and deed.
Keep a promise.
Find the time.
Forgo a grudge.
Forgive an enemy.
Listen.
Acknowledge any wrongdoing.
Try to understand.
Examine my demands on others.

Think of someone else first.
Be kind.
Be gentle.
Laugh a little.
Smile more.
Be happy.
Show my gratitude.
Welcome a stranger.
Speak your love.
Speak it again.
Live it again.
Life is a celebration!

*Instruct a wise man and he will be wiser still; teach a righteous man
and he will add to his learning.*   —*Prov. 9:9 NIV*

OPEN MIND

Higher Power, may I understand:
To be alert to my own needs, not to the faults of others;
To remain teachable;
To listen;
To keep an open mind; and
To learn not who's right but what's right.

*He who began a good work in you will carry it on to completion until
the day of Christ Jesus.*   —*Phil. 1:6 NIV*

DO IT NOW

Dear God,
I expect to pass through this world but once.
Any good thing, therefore, that I can do, or any kindness I can show
   to any fellow traveler, let me do it now.
Let me not defer nor neglect it, for I shall not pass this way again.

*Command them to do good, to be rich in good deeds, and to be generous
and willing to share. In this way they will lay up treasure for themselves
as a firm foundation for the coming age, so that they may take hold of
the life that is truly life.*   —*1 Tim. 6:18–19 NIV*

MY WORTH

I pray to remember that my worth is not determined by my show of outward strength, or the volume of my voice, or the thunder of my accomplishments. It is to be seen, rather, in terms of the nature and depth of my commitments, the genuineness of my friendships, the sincerity of my purpose, the quiet courage of my convictions, my capacity to accept life on life's terms, and my willingness to continue "growing up." This I pray.

Your beauty should not come from outward adornment, such as braided hair and the wearing of gold jewelry and fine clothes. Instead, it should be that of your inner self, the unfading beauty of a gentle and quiet spirit, which is of great worth in God's sight. —*1 Pet. 3:3–4 NIV*

Chapter Three

Prayers of Declaration

Statement of fact that we
emphasize to God about
ourselves and our daily lives.

*I said to the Lord, "You are my Lord: apart
from you I have no good thing."*
                          —Psalm 16:2 NIV

*P*rayers of declaration are statements of facts as we understand them. We declare in prayer what we want to emphasize to God about ourselves, our situations, our feelings, our progress, our relationships with God and others, and our lives in general.

Many of the prayers found in the Bible, especially the psalms, contain far more declarations to God than petitions for requests. The Bible shows examples of God's people telling him the way it is. The biblical figures prayed this way to apprise God of a situation or to remind God of a past covenant promise. The most celebrated of all biblical prayers of declaration is found in the familiar form of holy story.

The Jews would often prayerfully recite their holy story of God's deliverance from Egyptian bondage, his protection from Pharaoh's army, his miraculous opening of the Red Sea, his provision of food and water in the barren desert, his aid in crossing the Jordan at flood stage, his victorious power in the defeat of Jericho, his help in the domination and habitation of the promised land, and more. The Jews would always add to the holy story in an effort to bring it up to date. Once they had recited this prayer of declaration to God, they themselves would be encouraged about God's care and about his ability to see them through their present crises—whatever it might be. One of the best examples of the holy story is found in Nehemiah 9. If we take the time to read this and other passages, like Psalms 105, 106, and 136, we capture the feeling of a prayer of declaration.

Some of the psalms of David ask for nothing, give thanks for nothing, and offer no praise. These are prayers of declaration—psalms that only declare or report. Note how the 23rd Psalm states facts and contains no petition or praise. David basically announces, "The Lord is my shepherd and he takes good care of me!" We know David is directing this declaration to God when he says, "I will fear no evil, for you are with me."

How might we in recovery use a prayer of declaration? Like the Jews, we have our own holy story. It's about God's deliverance in our lives and his continued presence in our recovery. We can declare in prayer what God has done for us in the past and thereby gain confidence in what God will do for us in our present circumstances or crisis.

We can declare, as David did, the special ways we relate to God. Maybe seeing God as a shepherd doesn't fit our modern and urban mindset, but we might tell God that we see him as a loving and generous father. Or, as you will read in the first prayer of this section, we may see God as our ultimate sponsor. "The Lord is my sponsor. I shall not want. He maketh me to go to many meetings..."

We can also use prayers of declaration to report. Like a child who crawls onto Father's lap and talks about the day, we can tell our heavenly Father about our day, our moods, our activities, our relationships, and our concerns. We may even choose to tell God about current world and community events. He wants to hear from us. Just as one would call Mom to report life's details, we can call God. God awaits our call—our prayer.

The following prayers of declaration are statements of fact about life in recovery, and they are examples to help us create our own prayers of declaration to God.

Prayers of Declaration

THE 23RD ½ PSALM

The Lord is my sponsor! I shall not want.
He maketh me to go to many meetings.
He leadeth me to sit back, relax, and listen with an open mind.
He restoreth my soul, my sanity, and my health.
He leadeth me in the paths of sobriety, serenity, and fellowship
  for mine own sake.
He teacheth me to think, to take it easy, to live and let live, and
  to do first things first.
He maketh me honest, humble, and grateful.
He teacheth me to accept the things I cannot change, to change
  the things that I can, and giveth me the wisdom to know the
  difference.
Yea, though I walk through the valley of despair, frustration, guilt,
  and remorse, I will fear no evil, for thou art with me; the program, thy way of life, the Twelve Steps, they comfort me.
Thou prepares a table before me in the presence of mine enemies;
  rationalization, fear, anxiety, self-pity, and resentment. Thou
  anointest my confused mind and jangled nerves with knowledge, understanding, and hope. No longer am I alone; neither
  am I afraid, nor sick, nor helpless, nor hopeless. My cup runneth
  over.
Surely sobriety and serenity shall follow me every day of my life,
  twenty-four hours at a time, as I surrender my will to Thine and
  carry the message to others; and I will dwell in the house of my
  Higher Power, as I understand him, daily.
  Forever and ever.

*I am the good shepherd. The good shepherd lays down his life for the
sheep. I am the good shepherd; I know my sheep and my sheep know
me— .*
                                        —John 10:11,14 NIV

TODAY'S THOUGHT

Lord,
I am but one, but I am one;
I can't do everything,
But I can do *something;*
What I can do, I ought to do;
What I ought to do, God helping me,
I will do.

One man of you shall chase a thousand, for the Lord your God is he who fights for you, as he has promised you. —Josh. 23:10 NIV

THIS I BELIEVE

Tomorrow is yet to be.
But should God grant me another day,
    the hope, courage, and strength
    through the working of the Twelve Steps and Serenity Prayer,
    I shall be sufficiently provided for to meet my every need.
This I believe.

And my God will meet all your needs according to his glorious riches in Christ Jesus. —Phil. 4:19 NIV

NO GREATER POWER

To find direction and meaning, I must tap a Higher Power.
That Power is God as I understand him. I will start each day with
    God and take Steps Three, Seven, and Eleven. There is no Greater
    Power.
And then I will say:
    Lord, I turn my life and will over to you today.
    I will walk humbly with you and my fellow travelers.
    You are giving me a grateful heart for my many blessings.
    You are directing my thinking and separating me from self-pity,
    dishonesty, and self-seeking motives.
    You are removing my resentments, fears, and other character de-
    fects that stand in my way.
    You are giving me freedom from self-will.
    Your will, Lord, not mine.

You will show me today what I can do to help someone who is
still hurting.
As I go out today to do your bidding
you are helping me to become a better person.

I can do everything through him who gives me strength.

—Phil. 4:13 NIV

EVERY MORNING

Every morning I will rest my arms a while upon the windowsill of
heaven, gaze upon my Higher Power, and with that vision in my
heart, turn strong to meet my day.

My voice you shall hear in the morning, O Lord; in the morning I will
direct it to you, and I will look up.   *—Ps. 5:3 NKJV*

THE BEATITUDES

Blessed are the poor in spirit, for theirs in the kingdom of heaven.
Blessed are they that mourn, for they shall be comforted.
Blessed are the meek, for they shall inherit the earth.
Blessed are they that do hunger and thirst after righteousness,
    for they shall be filled.
Blessed are the merciful, for they shall obtain mercy.
Blessed are the pure in heart, for they shall see God.
Blessed are the peacemakers, for they shall be called the
    children of God.
Blessed are they that are persecuted for righteousness' sake,
    for theirs is the kingdom of heaven.

Set your minds on things above, not on earthly things.

—Col. 3:2 NIV

THE TWELVE STEPS PRAYER

Power, greater than myself, as I understand you, I willingly admit
that without your help, I am powerless over my dependencies and
my life has become unmanageable. I believe you can restore me to
sanity. I turn my life and my will over to you. I have made a searching and fearless moral inventory of myself; I admit to you, to myself,

and to another the exact nature of my wrongs. I am entirely ready to have you remove these defects of character. I humbly ask you to remove my shortcomings. I have made direct amends to all persons I have harmed, except when to do so would injure them or others. I will continue to take personal inventory, and when I am wrong, I will promptly admit it. I seek through prayer and meditation to improve my conscious contact with you and pray only for knowledge of your will for me and the power to carry it out.

Grant me the grace to carry the message of your help unto others and to practice the principles of the Twelve Steps in all my affairs.

The steps of a good man are ordered by the Lord, and he delights in his way. Though he fall, he shall not be utterly cast down, for the Lord upholds him with his hand. —*Ps. 37:23–24 NKJV*

GOD'S ANSWER

I asked you, God, for strength that I might achieve;
I was made weak that I might learn humbly to obey.
I asked for help that I might do greater things;
I was given infirmity that I might do better things.
I asked for riches that I might be happy;
I was given poverty that I might be wise.
I asked for power that I might have the praise of others;
I was given weakness that I might feel the need for you.
I asked for all things that I might enjoy life;
I was given life that I might enjoy all things.
No, dear Lord, I've gotten nothing that I asked for,
    but everything I had hoped for.
Despite myself, my prayers were answered,
    and I am among those most richly blessed.

When you ask, you do not receive, because you ask with wrong motives, that you may spend what you get on your pleasures [lusts].
—*James 4:3 NIV*

POSSIBILITIES PRAYER

I know, dear God, that my part in this program is going to be a thrilling and endless adventure. Despite all that has happened to me already, I know that I have just begun to grow. I have just begun to open to your love. I have just begun to touch the varied lives you are using me to change. I have just begun to sense the possibilities ahead. And these possibilities, I am convinced, will continue to unfold into ever new and richer adventures, not only for the rest of my reborn days but through eternity.

The path of the righteous is like the first gleam of dawn, shining ever brighter till the full light of day. —*Prov. 4:18 NIV*

SOBRIETY PRAYER

If I speak in the tongues of people and even of angels, but have not sobriety, I am a noisy gong or a clanging cymbal. And if I have prophetic powers and understand all mysteries and all knowledge, and if I have all faith so as to move mountains, but have not sobriety, I am nothing. If I give away all that I have, and if I deliver my body to be burned, but have not sobriety, I gain nothing.

When I am sober, I am patient and kind. When I am sober, I am not jealous, or boastful, or arrogant, or rude. When I am sober, I do not insist on my own way. When I am sober, I am not irritable or resentful. I do not rejoice at wrong as I used to do but rejoice in what is right.

When I am sober, I can bear all things, believe in all things, hope all things, and endure all things.

Sobriety never ends and never fails.

When I was using, I spoke like an arrogant child, thought like a stubborn child, and reasoned like a rebellious child. When I chose sobriety for my life, I gave up my childish ways.

So faith, hope, love, and sobriety abide. But for me, the most important has to be sobriety, for without it, I cannot have the other three, nor can I ever have the serenity I yearn to possess.

For by the grace given me I say to every one of you: Do not think of yourself more highly than you ought, but rather think of yourself with sober judgment, in accordance with the measure of faith God has given you. —*Rom. 12:3 NIV*

PRAYER FOR PROTECTION

The light of God surrounds me;
The love of God enfolds me;
The power of God protects me;
The presence of God watches over me;
Wherever I am, God is!

*The Lord is my light and my salvation—whom shall I fear? The Lord is
the strength of my life—of whom shall I be afraid?* —*Ps. 27:1 NIV*

NEW DAY

Thank you, God, for today.
This is the beginning of a new day. I can waste it or use it for
  good.
What I do today is important because I am exchanging a day of my
  life for it.
When tomorrow comes, this day will be gone forever—leaving in its
  place something I have traded for it.
I want it to be gain, not loss; good, not evil; success, not failure; in
  order that I shall not regret the price I paid for today.

Whatever you do, do it all for the glory of God. —*1 Cor. 10:31b NIV*

I PROMISE MYSELF!

Today I pray:
To promise myself to be so strong that nothing can disturb my peace
  of mind.
To talk health, happiness, and prosperity to every person   I
  meet.
To make all my friends feel that there is something in them.
To look at the sunny side of everything and make my optimism come
  true.
To think only of the best, to work only for the best, and expect only
  the best.
To be just as enthusiastic about the success of others as I am about
  my own.
To forget the mistakes of the past and press on to the greater
  achievements of the future.

To wear a cheerful countenance at all times and give every living creature I meet a smile.

To give so much time to the improvement of myself that I have no time to criticize others.

To be too large for worry, too noble for anger, too strong for fear, and too happy to permit the presence of trouble.

For as he thinks in his heart, so is he.   *—Prov. 23:7a NKJV*

RECOVERY PRAYER

Today and every day, I will be ever mindful that recovery is the most important thing in my life, without exception. I may believe my job, or my home life, or one of many other things, comes first. But if I don't stay with the program, chances are I won't have a job, a family, sanity, or even life. If I am convinced that everything in life depends on my recovery, I have a much better chance of improving my life. If I put other things first, I am only hurting my chances.

And they did not do as we expected, but they gave themselves first to the Lord and then to us in keeping with God's will.   *—2 Cor. 8:5 NIV*

Chapter Four

Prayers of Complaint

Cries of distress or complaints to God telling him where it hurts.

I pour out my complaint before him [God]; before him I tell my trouble.
                                    —Psalm 142:2 NIV

*G*od made us so that when we are hurt, we cry. From the day we were born, we have expressed our pain, sorrow, loss, discomfort, fear, and anger. Some of us express ourselves through tears, while others languish in silence and cry inwardly. Some loudly proclaim their hurt like an alarm, and still others hold their tears or anger until they're in the presence of a trusted friend. However we may express our pain, hurt, or discomfort, we have one thing in common; our God, our Higher Power, listens for our cry as surely as a mother attunes her ear to her baby's voice.

Can the one who made tears for our eyes and emotion for our souls not see and feel our hurt? Can the one who created ears for hearing and hearts for compassion not hear our cries and feel concern? God does see, he does feel, he does hear, he does care. He does want to know about our hurt, anger, frustration, and pain.

Prayers of complaint are our cries of distress. God is our trusted friend in whom we confide and with whom we share out hurt. When we complain to God, we tell him where it hurts. We understand that our complaint has reached out to the only one powerful enough to really help and heal.

Prayers of complaint are plentiful in the Book of Psalms and throughout Scripture. The patriarchs felt free to complain to God. Moses, in the earlier pages of Exodus, complained to God until God lost patience with the reluctant leader. Righteous Job, who had a lot to complain about, said, "I loathe my very life; therefore I will give free rein to my complaint and speak out [to God] in the bitterness of my soul." (Job 10:1 NIV)

Right after Job's angry complaint to God, one of Job's comforters rebuked him for speaking to God that way. But what Job had to say to God was quite in order, and God never chastised Job for his angry outburst. Like Job, many of us in recovery want to complain. We want to tell somebody how we hurt, we want to curse, and we want to tell God off sometimes. But most of us have "righteous" friends like Job's comforters. Ricky Righteousness and Sally Sanctimonious tell us to bite our tongues and swallow our hurt. But there is one person we can always complain to—God.

King David, "the sweet psalmist of Israel," not only sang sweet psalms of praise, but he also sang psalms and prayed prayers of complaint to God. When David was frightened by his enemies, he cried, "Hear me, O God, as I voice my complaint; protect my life from the threat of the enemy." (Ps. 64:1 NIV) When David had to hide in a cave, he prayed, "I pour out my complaint before him [God], before him I tell my trouble." (Ps. 142:2 NIV) When David was in deep anguish, he cried, "I am worn out from groaning; all night long I flood my bed with weeping and drench my couch with tears...[but]...the Lord has heard my cry." (Ps. 6:6-9 NIV) And when David didn't think God was paying attention to his pain, he screamed, "Awake, O Lord! Why do you sleep? Rouse yourself!" (Ps. 44:23 NIV)

Jesus expressed complaint in John 12 when his soul was troubled. He struggled and complained in the Garden of Gethsemane. Yes, he finally surrendered to God's will, but he felt the freedom to tell his Father of his hurt, apprehension, and inner struggle.

For those of us in recovery, the freedom to speak and pray honestly is very important. The Twelve-Step program has helped us to release our denial. Meetings have taught us to speak freely. Our fellows in recovery have supported our times of venting. And now, in prayers of complaint, we are free to tell God where it hurts.

For those who still believe that prayer ought to be saintly, sophisticated, shallow, or sweet, here is an excellent exercise: Read the Bible. The Bible does not hide the truth. The tears, the failures, the sins, and the humanity of all the men and women of God are open for all to see in the pages of Scripture.

The following prayers of complaint include Psalm 88 in its entirety. There is no positive upswing or moral to these prayers of complaint because that's not their purpose. Prayers of complaint are *expressions* of our sorrow, hurt, pain, frustration, and anger. The following prayers can help us become more comfortable with prayers of complaint and teach us how to pray honestly.

Prayers of Complaint

O Lord, the God who saves me, day and night I cry out before you.
May my prayer come before you; turn your ear to my cry.
For my soul is full of trouble and my life draws near the grave.
I am counted among those who go down to the pit; I am like a man
  without strength.
I am set apart with the dead, like the slain who lie in the grave,
  whom you remember no more, who are cut off from your care.
You have put me in the lowest pit, in the darkest depths.
Your wrath lies heavily upon me; you have overwhelmed me with
  all your waves.
You have taken from me my closest friends and have made me
  repulsive to them.
I am confined and cannot escape; my eyes are dim with grief.
I call to you, O Lord, every day; I spread out my hands to you.
Do you show your wonders to the dead? Do those who are dead
  rise up and praise you?
Is your love declared in the grave, your faithfulness in
  destruction?
Are your wonders known in the place of darkness, or your righteous
  deeds in the land of oblivion?
But I cry to you for help, O Lord; in the morning my prayer comes
  before you.
Why, O Lord, do you reject me and hide your face from me?
From my youth I have been afflicted and close to death; I have
  suffered your terrors and am in despair.
Your wrath has swept over me; your terrors have destroyed me.
All day long they surround me like a flood; they have completely
  engulfed me.
You have taken my companions and loved ones from me; the
  darkness is my closest friend.   —Ps. 88 NIV

A BEGINNER'S PRAYER

Lord, I want to love you, yet I am not sure.
I want to trust you, yet I am afraid of being taken in.
I know I need you, but I am ashamed of the need.
I want to pray, but I am afraid of being a hypocrite.
I need my independence, yet I fear to be alone.
I want to belong, yet I must be myself.
Take me, Lord, yet leave me alone.
Lord, I believe; help thou my unbelief.
O Lord, if you are there, you do understand, don't you?
Give me what I need, but leave me free to choose.
Help me work it out my own way, but don't let me go.
Let me understand myself, but don't let me despair.
Come unto me, O Lord, I want you there.
Lighten my darkness, but don't dazzle me.
Help me to see what I need to do, and give me strength to do it.
O Lord, I believe; help thou my unbelief.

Jesus asked the boy's father, "How long has he been like this?"
"From childhood," he answered. "It [the evil spirit] has often thrown
him into fire or water to kill him. But if you can do anything, take
pity on us and help us."
"If you can?" said Jesus. "Everything is possible for him who believes."
Immediately the boy's father exclaimed, "I do believe; help me overcome
my unbelief!" —Mark 9:21–24 NIV

LORD, I'M HURTING

Yes, Lord, I hurt.
The pain is deep,
    and I feel the mountains
    are so steep.
I cannot seem to stand.
Please, dear Lord,
    take my hand.
I cannot seem
    to find my way.
For me the sun
    is not shining today.
I know you're there;

I've felt your presence near.
But now, my Lord,
    my heart is gripped with fear.
Lord, help the sun to shine
    and to know
    that you are mine.
Heal this pain I feel;
    make your presence
    very real.
Today, Lord, I give you all.
Help me, dear Lord,
    not to fall.
And if I fall,
    hold me tight,
    so I can feel
    your strength and might.

*Then they cried out to the Lord in their trouble, and he delivered them
from their distress.* —Ps. 107:6 NIV

NO OTHER

I have no other helper than you;
    no other father,
    no other redeemer,
    no other support.
I pray to you.
Only you can help me.
My present misery is too great.
Despair grips me, and I am at my wit's end.
I am sunk in the depths, and I cannot pull myself up or out.
If it is your will, help me out of this misery.
Let me know that you are stronger than all misery and all enemies.
O Lord, if I come through this, please let the experience contribute
    to my and my contemporaries' blessing.
You will not forsake me; this I know.

*Answer me when I call to you, O my righteous God. Give me relief from
my distress; be merciful to me and hear my prayer.* —Ps. 4:1 NIV

Chapter Five

Prayers of Meditation

Listening-type prayers quiet our spirit
before God so we may draw near to him for
direction, inspiration, and fellowship.

*Whether you turn to the right or to the left,
your ears will hear a voice behind you, saying,
"This is the way; walk in it."*

—Isaiah 30:21 NIV

Prayers of meditation, popular with people in Twelve-Step recovery programs, are active listening prayers. In praying this way, we quiet our minds before God in order to draw near to him for direction, inspiration, and fellowship. This is one of the purest and most helpful forms of prayer in the Twelve-Step program. In fact, the commentary on the program's traditions states that prayer is "the raising of the heart and mind to God" (*Twelve Steps and Twelve Traditions Anonymous,* Alcoholics Anonymous World Services, Inc., 1953, p. 102)

In Christian circles, meditation has generally been understood to be a mental exercise, in which we focus our thoughts on some aspect of God. In other words, *we think* about his revelation, his word, his creation, our sinful nature, the glory of God, and our spiritual life. Thinking about these things is certainly laudatory and has a place in our prayer life. Yet, something else is required.

Many of us find it nearly impossible to sit quietly before God in solitude and serenity. We treat God just like we treat the rest of our lives. We live with a sort of mental torment and emotional pain that keeps us searching for distractions, painkillers, and noise. Many of us complain about the voices of the "committee" in our heads, those internal voices that shame and condemn us, extol us to be more, to be better, to be perfect.

The committee won't let us accept ourselves as we are. Our internal voices need to either judge or reason and figure out why we feel like we do. The last thing the committee wants to let us do is feel our feelings. So we turn on the radio as soon as we get in the car; leave the television on even when no one is watching; work, play, and socialize at a killing pace so the silence can't catch us off guard and let us feel our pain.

Yet to really experience communion with ourselves or with God, we need to experience our whole existence, in silent meditative prayerfulness. This sort of praying feeds our serenity.

To pray prayers of meditation, we must learn to disengage our minds and reengage our spirits. One way to do this is to use the technique of repeating a simple phrase, or a mantra, over and over again. The mantra or meditative prayer is simple spiritual prayer that accomplishes many things. The repetition of a single word, a sung expression, or a simple spiritual phrase—for instance, The Jesus Prayer, "Lord, Jesus Christ, have mercy on me"—can clear our minds. By the repetition, we bypass our overused mental mode. We get out of thinking too much.

Once our active mind is silenced, our spiritual sense is awakened. By giving up conversation with God, trying to tell him our thoughts, we can open ourselves for the Spirit to enter our lives. The Apostle Paul said it this way:

> In the same way, the Spirit helps us in our weakness. We do not know what we ought to pray for, but the Spirit himself intercedes for us *with groans that words cannot express*. And he who searches our hearts knows the mind of the Spirit, because the Spirit intercedes for the saints *in accordance with God's will*. (Rom. 8:26–27 NIV; author emphasis)

This listening prayer declares our poverty before God and invites God's grace into our lives. It creates a childlike attitude of trust. We can give up trying to figure things out and more readily receive the kingdom—God's rulership and will. When we purposely give up thinking, we can start listening to God.

The following commonly used Christian mantras are offered as examples. Also included is an inspirational reading and a prayer regarding meditation.

Prayers of Meditation

THE JESUS PRAYER

Lord, Jesus Christ, have mercy on me.

SURRENDER

Not my will, but thine be done.

WORDS OF PRAISE

Hallelujah.

Praise you, Lord

Glory to your name.

SPIRITUAL PHRASES

Glory be to the Father, the Son, and to the Holy Spirit.

Praise God from whom all blessings flow.

Amazing grace, how sweet the sound.

I pray for the peace that passes understanding.

Jesus (or God), be with me now and always.

Thy will be done.

Let go, let God.

My Jesus, have mercy.

Oh, Jesus, save me.

All for thee, most Sacred Heart of Jesus.
Grant, our Lord, that I may know thy will and do it.

Stay with me Lord, the day is now far spent.

Oh, Lord, hear my prayer.

THE PEACE OF MEDITATION

So we may know God better
and feel his quiet power,
let us daily keep in silence
a meditation hour.

For to understand God's greatness
and to use his gifts each day,
the soul must learn to meet him
in a meditative way.

For our Father tells his children
that if they would know his will,
they must seek him in the silence
when all is calm and still.

For nature's greatest forces
are found in quiet things,
like softly falling snowflakes
drifting down on angels' wings,

or petals dropping soundlessly
from a lovely full-blown rose.
God comes closest to us
when our souls are in repose,

so let us plan with prayerful care
to always allocate
a certain portion of each day
to be still and meditate.

In the same way, the Spirit helps us in our weakness. We do not know what we ought to pray for, but the Spirit himself intercedes for us with groans that words cannot express. And he who searches our hearts knows the mind of the Spirit, because the Spirit intercedes for the saints in accordance with God's will. —*Rom. 8:26–27 NIV*

SELF-RESPECT PRAYER

O God, teach me that self-respect cannot be hunted. It cannot be purchased. It is never for sale. It comes to me when I am alone, in quiet moments, in quiet places, when I suddenly realize that, knowing the good, I have done it; knowing the beautiful, I have served it; knowing the truth, I have spoken it.

He who pursues righteousness and love finds life, prosperity, and honor. —*Prov. 21:21 NIV*

Chapter Six

Prayers of Submission

Responses through submission or surrender to God's guidance, direction, and right to rule.

"My Father, if it is not possible for this cup to be taken away unless I drink it, may your will be done." —*Matthew 26:42 NIV*

$\mathcal{I}$n a prayer of submission, we respond, through submission or surrender, to God's guidance or direction, to God's revealed will, to God's specific instruction, to God's written word (the Bible), to God's appointed authority (our leadership and law) to God's control over our life and its circumstances, and/or to God's right to rule. When Jesus was in the Garden of Gethsemane, he struggled with his Father's will for a time in prayer. But ultimately, he came to a place of acceptance and submission before the Father. He demonstrated that submission in a simple yet honest prayer of surrender: "My Father, if it is not possible for this cup to be taken away unless I drink it, may your will be done." (Matt. 26:42 NIV)

When Mary, the mother of Jesus, heard the message that she had been chosen by God to bear the Messiah without the aid of any man, she responded with a prayer of submission, "I am the Lord's servant. … May it be to me as you have said." (Luke 1:38 NIV) The great Prophet Samuel's first submissive response to God came when he was a child growing up in the temple. God spoke to Samuel in the night. And with a simple prayer of submission, "Speak, for your servant is listening." (1 Sam. 3:10 NIV), Samuel began a lifetime of surrender to God's will.

The Prophet Isaiah prayed a prayer of submission for the entire nation when Israel's rebellion prevented their proper response. Isaiah prayed, "Yet, O Lord, you are our Father. We are the clay, you are the potter; we are all the work of your hand." (Isa. 64:8 NIV) Isaiah's prayer is a masterful example of the incorporation of poetic style in prayer. The beauty and art of well-chosen words make the prayer no less a surrendering to God's will.

Throughout the pages of Scripture we find God's people being confronted with God's will for their lives. Often these people struggled with God's plan, as did Moses, Gideon, and Jeremiah; but in the end, they each responded and prayerfully surrendered and submitted to God's will.

But what about us—believers who are in recovery and who use the Twelve Steps? We don't pretend to be great like the Virgin Mary, Moses, or Isaiah. We do, however, understand the value of submissive prayer. It is a vital form of prayer for those of us who are being healed by God's grace and governance, and progress in recovery requires an attitude of prayerful submission and surrender. In fact, unlike most other forms of prayer, prayers of surrender are an essential component in each of the Twelve Steps.

In Step One, we breathe an exhausted yet expectant prayer of surrender as we quit trying to manage and control our own lives. Step Two and its faith in a Higher Power is not even possible unless we surrender ourselves with faith. Step Three is clearly the time to surrender in prayer as we make a decision to turn our will and our lives over to the care of God.

In Step Four, we surrender our denial before God and submit to the reality of our moral defects. Step Five calls us to submit to God's healing work through confession. Step Six calls us to submit to God's inner working in our lives as he makes us ready to release our defects. Step Seven is impossible without a submissive spirit to foster humility. Steps Eight and Nine require a deliberate act of surrender to God's will as we make amends. Step Ten requires our submission to a continual process before God. Step Eleven brings us face to face with the primacy of God's will in our lives and the need to submit to it. And finally, Step Twelve calls us to surrender as we submit to the Twelve-Step principles in all our affairs and as we submit to the call to carry this message to others.

The following prayers of submission are provided as examples to use in developing our own prayers of surrender and submission to God.

Prayers of Submission

MY FIRST PRAYER

I surrender to you my entire life,
　O God of my understanding.
I have made a mess of it
　trying to run it myself.
You take it, the whole thing,
　and run it for me,
　according to your will and plan.

*Teach me to do your will, for you are my God; may your good Spirit lead
me on level ground.*　　　　　　　　　　　　—Ps. 143:10 NKJV

THE FELLOWSHIP PRAYER

Dear Higher Power, I am grateful that:
I am part of the fellowship, one among many, but I am one.
I need to work the steps for the development of the buried life
　within me.
Our program may be human in its organization, but it is divine in
　its purpose. The purpose is to continue my spiritual awakening.
Participating in the privileges of the movement, I shall share in the
　responsibilities, taking it upon myself to carry my fair share of the
　load, not grudgingly, but joyfully.
To the extent that I fail in my responsibilities, the program fails.
To the extent that I succeed, the program succeeds.
I shall not wait to be drafted for service to my fellow member. I shall
　volunteer.
I shall be loyal in my attendance, generous in my giving, kind
　in my criticism, creative in my suggestions, and loving in my
　attitudes.
I shall give to the program my interest, my enthusiasm, my devotion,
　and most of all … myself.

But Ruth replied, *"Don't urge me to leave you or to turn back from you.
Where you go I will go, and where you stay I will stay. Your people will
be my people and your God my God. Where you die I will die, and there
I will be buried. May the Lord deal with me, be it ever so severely, if
anything but death separates you and me."* —Ruth 1:16–17 NIV

THE RIGHT ROAD

Dear God,
I have no idea where I am going.
I do not see the road ahead of me.
I cannot know for certain where it will end.
Nor do I really know myself.
But I believe this:
I believe that the desire to please you does, in fact, please you.
I hope I have that desire in everything I do.
I hope I never do anything apart from that desire.
And I know that if I do this you will lead me by the right road,
    though I may know nothing about it at the time.
Therefore, I will trust you always, for though I may seem to be lost
    and in the shadow of death, I will not be afraid, because I know
    you will never leave me to face my troubles alone.

*He tends his flock like a shepherd: He gathers the lambs in his arms and
carries them close to his heart; he gently leads those that have young.*
—Isa. 40:11 NIV

AM I WILLING?

Dear Higher Power, help me:
To forget what I have done for other people, and to remember what
    other people have done for me.
To ignore what the world owes me, and to think what I owe the
    world.
To put my rights in the background, and my duties in the middle
    distance, and my chances to do a little more than my duty in the
    foreground.
To see that my fellow members are just as real as I am, and to try to
    look behind their faces to their hearts, as hungry for joy as mine is.
To own that probably the only good reason for my existence is not
    what I can get out of life but what I can give to life.

To close my book of complaints against the management of the universe and look for a place where I can sow a few seeds of happiness—am I willing to do these things even for a day?
Then I have a good chance of staying with the program.

*Then I heard the voice of the Lord saying, "Whom shall I send? And
who will go for us?" And I said, "Here am I. Send me!" And he said,
"Go."*   —*Isa. 6:8–9a NIV*

THE WAY

Dear Lord, today I pray:
The way is long,
   let us go together.
The way is difficult,
   let us help each other.
The way is joyful,
   let us share it.
The way is ours alone,
   let us go in love.
The way grows before us,
let us begin.

But he who unites himself with the Lord is one with him in spirit.
                                              —*1 Cor. 6:17 NIV*

LET GO, LET GOD

Higher Power, help me to understand:
To "let go" does not mean to stop caring; it means I can't do it for
   someone else.
To "let go" is not to enable but to allow learning from natural
   consequences.
To "let go" is to admit powerlessness, which means the outcome is
   not in my hands.
To "let go" is not to try to change or blame another; it's to make the
   most of myself.
To "let go" is not to care for but to care about.
To "let go" is not to fix but to be supportive.
To "let go" is not to judge but to allow another to be a human
   being.

To "let go" is not to protect, but to permit another to face reality.

To "let go" is not to deny but to accept.

To "let go" is not to nag, scold, or argue but instead to search out my own shortcomings and correct them.

To "let go" is not to adjust everything to my desire but to take each day as it comes and cherish myself in it.

Trust in the Lord with all your heart and lean not on your own understanding. —*Prov. 3:5 NIV*

Chapter Seven

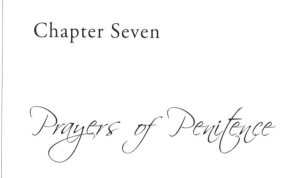

Requests for help to discern and search out our faults; expressions of sorrow for our shortcomings; prayers of confession, admission, repentance, and prayers for mercy.

Search me, O God, and know my heart; test me and know my anxious thoughts. See if there is any offensive way in me, and lead me in the way everlasting. —Psalm 139:23–24 NIV

Once our denial begins to fade, we recognize that we are powerless to control and manage life. Once we admit to the possibility of faults, defects, and shortcomings in our lives, we can begin to sincerely pray prayers of penitence. The earliest form of prayers of penitence are the Step Four type prayers that solicit God's searching help.

King David of Israel declared in Psalm 19:12, "Who can discern his errors?" In his familiar Psalm 139, David prayed, "Search me, O God, and know my heart; test me and know my anxious thoughts. See if there is any offensive way in me, and lead me in the way everlasting." Our first prayers of penitence are understanding prayers that ask God to point out our sins and shortcomings.

Prayers of penitence move from the place of searching for sin to the place expressing sorrow and regret for the sins, defects, and shortcomings that God has uncovered and brought to our attention. When the Prophet Nathan uncovered David's adultery with Bathsheba and the murder of Uriah, David expressed great sorrow. And when the baby born of David and Bathsheba's sin was dying, David fasted and mourned for days.

After the Apostle Peter denied Christ three times in the courtyard of the temple, a rooster crowed revealing Peter's sin. That revelation of sin brought Peter great remorse. The Bible says, "Then Peter remembered the word Jesus had spoken: 'Before the rooster crows, you will disown me three time.' And he [Peter] went outside and wept bitterly." (Matt. 26:75 NIV)

When we finally face ourselves and our sins, it's okay to express our sorrow, regret, and remorse to God in prayers of penitence. Many of us have damaged the lives of others as David did. Many of us have lost some of the precious years of our children's childhood. Sin's effect is destructive and painful. And we have destroyed and wasted years of our own lives. It's appropriate to express remorse to God.

When we pray prayers of penitence, sometimes it's easy to hide in our "just a dirty, rotten, sinner" mode. In this mode or mind-set we say, "I don't need to confess specifically. I'm all bad. My whole life is a mess. I'm just a dirty, rotten, sinner—all of me is rotten to the bone." So long as we see ourselves as all bad, and confess only in general, we will never begin to deal with the specific hindrances and enduring defects of our lives. We must seek God's help in being specific in our Step Four inventory and in being specific in our Step Five penitent prayer of confession.

After expressing our remorse, we should pray penitent prayers of confession and admission. These are in essence Step Five prayers because we admit to God the exact nature of our wrongs which we became aware of in Step Four. The important words here are "the exact nature of our wrongs." God has (if we have asked him) pointed out our sin by his searching Spirit and we have admitted and confessed our wrongs to God. If we are working Step Ten on a regular basis, then we confess what God shows us daily.

Penitent prayers of repentance are Step Six prayers. Step Six says that we "were entirely ready to have God remove all these defects of character." That willingness implies a change of mind—a desire to move beyond emotional remorse and sorrow. We move to a place of right thinking, where we want a change that involves the removal of our defects.

Penitent prayers for mercy and forgiveness are Step Seven prayers. Step Seven says that we "humbly asked him [God] to remove our shortcomings." We want forgiveness and the cleansing of our sins and shortcomings. David prayed for this in Psalm 51: "Have mercy on me, O God, according to your unfailing love; according to your great compassion blot out my transgression. Wash away all my iniquity and cleanse me from my sin."

Humility characterizes Step Seven prayers of penitence as we ask for forgiveness and mercy. Jesus told a parable of two sinners: a Pharisee and a tax collector. Jesus said that the Pharisee proudly boasted before God about his righteousness instead of being humbled by his sin and instead of seeing himself as God did. The tax collector, however, knew he was a sinner. Jesus said that he couldn't even lift his eyes to heaven; instead, he beat his breast and humbly cried, "God, have mercy on me, a sinner." Jesus said, "I tell you that this man, rather than the other [the Pharisee], went home justified before God. For everyone who exalts himself will be humbled, and he who humbles himself will be exalted." (Luke 18:14 NIV)

The following prayers are provided to help us approach God in penitence. They are intended as aids and examples in developing our own prayer lives. Our individual shortcomings, sins, defects, and wrongs must be sought out, confessed, repented of, and forgiven. Let us make our prayers specific and personal.

Prayers of Penitence

LIGHT A CANDLE

O God of my understanding,
light a candle within my heart,
that I may see what is therein and
remove the wreckage of the past.

*Search me, O God, and know my heart; test me and know my anxious
thoughts. See if there is any offensive way in me, and lead me in the way
everlasting.* —*Ps. 139:23–24 NIV*

TO BE HONEST

Higher Power, help me to be honest with myself.
It is so easy to alibi, to make excuses for my shortcomings.
It is so easy to blame others and circumstances as a child does.
Help me to see myself honestly; a human being who needs you this
    day and every day.
Help me to surrender my weak will to your strength.

Hear, O Lord, and be merciful to me; O Lord, be my help.
                                       —*Ps. 30:10 NIV*

NEW BEGINNINGS

O Lord, by the Holy Spirit's fair and loving search
    and by Christ's redemptive and cleansing work,
    purge our lives of all defects and sin.
Help us to be honest with ourselves and ruthless with our
    shortcomings.
Thus may we be enabled to accept your wonderful gift of *new
beginnings* and live in the joyous assurance of your pardon
    and peace.
Amen.

Who may ascend the hill of the Lord? Who may stand in his holy place?
He who has clean hands and a pure heart. —*Ps. 24:3–4a* NIV

PRAYER FOR HEALING

Higher Power,
You have told us to ask and we will receive, to seek and we will find,
   to knock and you will open the door to us.
I trust in your love for me and in the healing power of your
   compassion. I praise you and thank you for the mercy you have
   shown to me.
Higher Power, I am sorry for all my mistakes. I ask for your help in
   removing the negative patterns my of life. I accept with all my
   heart your forgiving love.
And I ask for the grace to be aware of the character defects that exist
   within myself. Let me not offend you by my weak human nature
   or by my impatience, resentment, or neglect of people who are a
   part of my life. Rather, teach me the gift of understanding and
   the ability to forgive, just as you continue to forgive me.
I seek your strength and your peace so that I may become your
   instrument in sharing those gifts with others.
Guide me in my prayer that I might know what needs to be healed
   and how to ask you for that healing.
It is you, Higher Power, whom I seek. Please enter the door of my
   heart and fill me with the presence of your spirit now and forever.
I thank you, God, for doing this.

"Those whom I love I rebuke and discipline. So be earnest, and repent.
Here I am! I stand at the door and knock. If anyone hears my voice and
opens the door, I will come in and eat with him, and he with me."
                                                     —*Rev. 3:19–20* NIV

ALL THAT WE OUGHT

All that we ought to have thought and have not thought,
All that we ought to have said and have not said,
All that we ought to have done and have not done;
All that we ought not to have thought and yet have thought,
All that we ought not to have spoken and yet have spoken,
All that we ought not to have done and yet have done;

For thoughts, words, and works, pray we, O God, for forgiveness,
And repent with penance.

Wash away all my iniquity and cleanse me from my sin.

—Ps. 51:2 NIV

WHO, ME?

I need to be forgiven, Lord, so many times a day.
So often do I stumble and fall. Be merciful, I pray.
Help me not be critical when others' faults I see.
For so often, Lord, the same faults are in me.

*Be kind and compassionate to one another, forgiving each other, just as
in Christ God forgave you.*   *—Eph. 4:32 NIV*

TRUE POWER

Take from me, Higher Power, my false pride and grandiosity, all
my phoniness and self-importance, and help me find the courage
that shows itself in gentleness, the wisdom that shows itself in
simplicity, and the true power that shows itself in modesty and
humility.

*But he gives us more grace. That is why Scripture says: "God opposes the
proud but gives grace to the humble."*   *—James 4:6 NIV*

HUMILITY PRAYER

Lord, I am far too much influenced by what people think of me;
which means that I am always pretending to be either richer or
smarter than I really am. Please prevent me from trying to attract
attention.

Don't let me gloat over praise on the one hand and be discouraged
by criticism on the other, nor let me waste time weaving the most
imaginary situations in which the heroic, charming, witty person
present is myself.

Show me how to be humble of heart.

Therefore, whoever humbles himself like this little child is the greatest in the kingdom of heaven. —*Matt. 18:4 NIV*

CHANGE ME

Life has humbled me, God. Pain has brought me down. Powerlessness, unmanageability, shortcomings, and sin—all these mark my life now, but I choose to lay aside all pride, to bow before you, and to cry, "Change me."

Humble yourselves before the Lord, and he will lift you up.
—*James 4:10 NIV*

RELEASE ME

Lord, keep me from the habit of thinking I must say something on every subject and on every occasion.

Release me from wanting to control everybody's affairs.

Keep my mind free from the recital of endless details—give me wings to get to the point.

I ask for grace enough to listen to the tales of others' pains. Help me to endure them with patience, but seal my lips on my own aches and pains—they are increasing, and my love of rehearsing them is becoming sweeter as the years go by.

Teach me the glorious lesson that occasionally it is possible that I may be mistaken.

Keep me reasonably sweet. I do not want to be a saint—some of them are so hard to live with—but a sour old person is one of the crowning works of the devil.

Give me the ability to see good things in unexpected places and talents in unexpected people. And give me, O Lord, the grace to tell them so.

Make me thoughtful, but not moody; helpful, but not bossy. With my vast store of wisdom, it seems a pity not to use it all, but you know, Lord, that I want a few friends at the end.

"I am coming soon. Hold on to what you have, so that no one will take your crown." —*Rev. 3:11 NIV*

FIRST THINGS FIRST

Dear Higher Power, remind me:
To tidy up my own mind,
To keep my sense of values straight,
To sort out the possible and the impossible,
To turn the impossible over to you,
And get busy on the possible.

*Therefore gird up the loins of your mind, be sober, and rest your hope
fully upon the grace that is to be brought to you at the revelation of
Christ Jesus.* —1 Pet. 1:13 NKJV

LEAD ME AND GUIDE ME

Almighty God, I humbly pray,
Lead me and guide me through this day.
Cast out my selfishness and sin,
Open my heart to let you in.
Help me now as I blindly stray
Over the pitfalls along the way.
Let me have courage to face each task,
Invest me with patience and love, I ask.
Care for me through each hour today,
Strengthen and guard me now, I pray.

As I forgive, forgive me too,
Needing your mercy as I do.
Oh give me your loving care,
Never abandon me to despair.
Yesterday's wrongs I would seek to right,
Make me more perfect in your sight.
Oh teach me to live as best I can,
Use me to help my fellow man.
Save me from acts of bitter shame,
    I humbly ask it in your name.

*Since you are my rock and my fortress, for the sake of your name lead
and guide me.* —Ps. 31:3 NIV

Chapter Eight

Prayers of Imprecation

Prayers that seek God's deliverance from and judgment on the enemies in our lives.

Contend, O Lord, with those who contend with me; fight against those who fight against me.
—Psalm 35:1 NIV

$\mathcal{L}$ike prayers of complaint, imprecatory prayers are abundant in the Old Testament's Book of Psalms. And like prayers of penitence, imprecatory prayers seek God's aid in our deliverance from forces greater than ourselves. The Lord Jesus taught us to pray, "forgive us our trespasses," but he also taught us to say, "deliver us from evil."

Like prayers of complaint, imprecatory prayers are not often prayed by Ricky Righteousness or Sarah Sanctimonious. They prefer that we pray sanitary prayers that ignore the presence or possibility of enemies. However, in the real world, there is a real Satan and a fallen nature within each of us that is bent toward evil.

David prayed this imprecatory prayer about evil within his own city and community:

> Confuse the wicked, O Lord, confound their speech, for I see violence and strife in the city.
> Day and night they prowl about on its walls; malice and abuse are within it.
> Destructive forces are at work in the city; threats and lies never leave its streets. (Ps. 55:9–11 NIV)

In another place he prayed against his enemies: "Contend, O Lord, with those who contend with me; fight against those who fight against me." (Ps. 35:1 NIV) This entire Psalm is a prayer of imprecation.

Anyone familiar with the Book of Psalms knows how plentiful

these imprecatory prayers are. And anyone who has thoughtfully considered these Psalms has also wondered about the brutal nature of Psalms like 109 and 137. But evil must be honestly faced, confronted, and dealt with in God's power. We must remember the old proverb: "Evil triumphs when good people do nothing." During the twelve-year rule of Hitler, the German church stood silent, and six million Jews were exterminated.

Consider for a moment what Jeremiah said when confronted with evil in an interesting passage found in the book that bears his name:

> "Because the Lord revealed their plot to me, I knew it, for at that time he showed me what they were doing. I had been like a gentle lamb led to the slaughter; I did not realize that they had plotted against me, saying, 'Let us destroy the tree and its fruit; let us cut him off from the land of the living, that his name be remembered no more.' But, O Lord Almighty, you who judge righteously and test the heart and mind, let me see your vengeance upon them, for to you I have committed my cause." (Jer. 11:18–20 NIV)

In this passage, Jeremiah uncovers the plot of his enemies, and then he prays an imprecatory prayer for God's vengeance.

Even Jesus and the Apostle Paul prayed imprecatory prayers. Paul became harsh at times. In the Book of Galatians, chapter five, Paul cursed the agitators who troubled the church and insisted on circumcision. And Jesus once cursed a fruitless tree:

> Early in the morning, as he was on his way back to the city, he was hungry. Seeing a fig tree by the road, he went up to it but found nothing on it except leaves. Then he said to it, "May you never bear fruit again!" immediately the tree withered. (Matt. 21:18–19 NIV)

The enemies that torment us may not necessarily be spiritual forces or human agents outside ourselves. Our greatest foes may be forces that operate within us—the craving for alcohol or drugs, the compulsion to abuse ourselves or others, or addictive/compulsive behaviors that cause depression, fear, doubt, and many other disorders.

We need prayers of imprecation in order to seek God's help against the powerful enemies in our lives that seek to control and dominate us. It is appropriate and advantageous to pray prayers like, "O God, please fight against this destructive anger (or whatever) that dwells within my heart and wants to consume me. I am powerless under its grasp. But you, O Lord, are able to destroy it. Root it out. Deliver me from it."

Imprecatory prayers are always directed to God, who is being invoked to come to our aid. We never directly curse another, nor do we directly curse Satan. Even Michael the archangel did not directly curse the devil when confronted in a struggle. Jude says, "But ever the archangel Michael, when he was disputing with the devil about the body of Moses, did not dare to bring a slanderous accusation against him but he said, 'The Lord rebuke you!'" (Jude 9) Even if we wanted to, it is not within our power to curse anyone or anything. So we pray and entrust it to God. Step One has taught us that.

There are not many written prayers of imprecation apart from the pages of Scripture, and there are even fewer imprecatory prayers written from a Twelve-Step perspective. So only Psalm 35 and a few written prayers are provided here. By using them and our own experiences, we can develop our own specific prayers of imprecation against the enemies in our lives.

Prayers of Imprecation

Contend, O Lord, with those who contend with me;
fight against those who fight against me.

Take up shield and buckler;
arise and come to my aid.

Brandish spear and javelin against those who pursue me.
Say to my soul, "I am your salvation."

May those who seek my life be disgraced and put to shame;
may those who plot my ruin by turned back in dismay.

May they be like chaff before the wind,
with the angel of the Lord driving them away;

May their path be dark and slippery,
with the angel of the Lord pursuing them.

Since they hid their net for me without cause and without cause dug a
pit for me, may ruin overtake them by surprise—may they fall in to the
pit, to their ruin.

Then my soul will rejoice in the Lord
and delight in his salvation.

My whole being will exclaim, "Who is like you, O Lord?
You rescue the poor from those too strong for them,
the poor and needy from those who rob them."

—Ps. 35:1–10 NIV

LITANY

When I am overwhelmed by the compulsion to (manipulate circumstances, blame, drink, use drugs, hurt myself or others—name your specific compulsion),

Response: Deliver me from this evil, dear God.

When I want to meet anger by (lashing out, hitting, name calling, escaping and running away—name your specific temptation),

Response: Deliver me from this evil, dear God.

When I try to make (money, people, booze, drugs, the Church— name your specific false God) into God,

Response: Deliver me from this evil, dear God.

When others try to control me through (manipulation, promises or false security, abuse, misused authority—name your own situation),

Response: Deliver me from this evil, dear God.

Dogs have surrounded me;
a band of evil men has encircled me,
they have pierced my hands and my feet.
I can count all my bones;
people stare and gloat over me.
They divide my garments among them
and cast lots for my clothing.
But you, O Lord, be not far off;
O my Strength, come quickly to help me.
Deliver my life from the sword,
my precious life from the power of the dogs.

—Ps. 22:16–20 NIV

DELIVER ME

My Father, who art in heaven,
deliver me from evil down here.
Enemies from within torment
and fill me with doubts and fear.

Forces beyond my controlling
overpower me and rob me of peace.
They strip me of sanity and pleasure
and leave me hurting and weak.

Past mistakes, present failures haunt me.
The committee convenes to condemn.
I'm torn by my fears and emotions;
O Lord, make this nightmare soon end.

I call out your name for deliverance,
and cry out to you for release.
Destroy the foes that enslave me,
Lord, crush their power—defeat.

You alone are my help, my deliverer;
In no one else do I dare trust.
Hear me now and avenge me, I pray;
come now to my aid—please rush.

I pledge to honor and praise you
when my spirit is again released.
I'll tell of your wondrous salvation,
when my spirit again knows sweet peace.

Arise, O Lord!
  Deliver me, O my God!
Strike all my enemies on the jaw;
  break the teeth of the wicked.
From the Lord comes deliverance.
  May your blessing be on your people.   —Ps. 3:7–8 NIV

RIGHT LIVING

Higher Power, deliver me:
From the cowardice that dares not face new truth;
From the laziness that is contented with half-truth;
From the arrogance that thinks it knows all truth.
These things, good Lord, that I pray for
Give me the strength to work for.

I call to the Lord, who is worthy of praise, and I am saved from my enemies. —Ps. 18:3 NIV

AGAINST TEMPTATIONS

May the strength of my Higher Power guide me.
May the power of God preserve me.
May the wisdom of my Higher Power instruct me.
May the hand of God protect me.
May the way of God direct me.
May the shield of God defend me.
And may the presence of, and belief in, my Higher Power guard
  me against the temptations of the world.

He guides the humble in what is right and teaches them in his way. —Ps. 25:9 NIV

Chapter Nine

Prayers of Intercession

Prayers that we pray on behalf of others.

We always thank God, the Father of our Lord Jesus Christ, when we pray for you.
—Colossians 1:3 NIV

*I*ntercession is another very common type of prayer. Scripture abounds with prayers of intercession. Noah, the ancient preacher of righteousness, interceded for the lost world that was doomed for destruction. Abraham prayed for Lot and his family in Sodom. Moses constantly prayed for the rebellious and unruly children of Israel. At one point God was going to destroy the children of Israel and make a new nation from Moses, but Moses interceded and prayed, "O Lord, why should your anger burn against your people, who you brought out of Egypt with great power and a mighty hand?" (Exod. 32:11 NIV) God relented at Moses' prayer, and Israel was saved.

One reason to intercede for others is to help them avert judgment. All of us in Twelve-Step recovery programs know others who have not yet found the tools for recovery and who have not yet called out to God for help. We pray for them because judgment—the consequence of their own choices—is coming to them. We pray for these people as others prayed for us.

Joshua interceded for all of Israel with a complaint when Israel's army was defeated at Ai: "Ah, Sovereign Lord, why did you ever bring this people across the Jordan to deliver us into the hands of the Amorites to destroy us? If only we had been content to stay on the other side of the Jordan!" (Josh. 7:7 NIV)

We have all watched another—perhaps someone dear to us—struggle with hardships that seem to destine them to failure and loss. It is appropriate to complain to God on their behalf. We might pray, "Why, O Lord, have you allowed my friend to suffer such hardship and abuse? His life is a struggle already. Now insult is added to injury. Open your eyes to his pain. Help him."

King Jehoshaphat interceded for his people with imprecatory prayer when an enemy threatened. He prayed, "O our God, will you not judge them? For we have no power to face this vast army that is attacking us. We do not know what to do, but our eyes are upon you." (2 Chron. 20:12 NIV) When we see enemies attacking our loved ones, family, and friends, we can intercede with prayers of imprecation for them and pray for God to defeat the enemies that threaten them.

Daniel interceded for Israel with penitent prayer. Israel was in captivity because of sin when Daniel prayed, "O Lord, the great and awesome God, who keeps his covenant of love with all who love him and obey his commands, we have sinned and done wrong. We have been wicked and have rebelled; we have turned away from your commands and laws." (Dan. 9:4–5 NIV) God heard Daniel's prayer and began to work for Israel's restoration.

We cannot confess someone else's sins and be assured that God will forgive, but we can humble ourselves in the place of our country, community, companions, or contenders, asking for God's mercy, compassion, and forgiveness. As Jesus hung on the cross, he prayed that God might forgive his executioners who were acting in ignorance. Stephen, the first Christian martyr, made a similar request as he was being stoned.

In John 17, in a lengthy prayer of declaration and intercession, Jesus prayed for his disciples and their protection: "My prayer is not that you take them out of the world but that you protect them from the evil one." He prayed for their sanctification: "Sanctify them by the truth, your word is truth." And he prayed for their unity: "… that all of them may be one, Father, just as you are in me and I am in you. May they also be in us so that the world may believe that you have sent me."

From Jesus' example we too are encouraged to pray for one another's protection, sanctification (dedication and purity), and unity. We all know former program members who have fallen away or backslidden, for whom we can pray. We can also pray for those of us who remain in the program and continue to recover.

Last and most important among the biblical expressions of intercession is the prayer for God's will. The Apostle Paul interceded for the Colossians' church with God's will in mind. He wrote to them and said, "…since the day we heard about you, we have not stopped praying for you and asking God to fill you with the knowledge of his will through all spiritual wisdom and understanding." (Col. 1:9 NIV) Like Paul, we have personally learned how important it is for us to pray for personal knowledge of God's will for ourselves. And now we understand how important that knowledge is for others. So we pray, "God, show them your will."

In essence, nearly every prayer that is appropriate for ourselves can also be prayed for another. The following prayers of intercession can encourage our own specific prayers for family, friends, program members, and others for whom we care. Also included are some inspirational prayers that direct our focus toward others.

Prayers for Intercession

THE VICTIMS OF ADDICTION

O blessed Lord, you ministered to all who came to you.

Look with compassion upon all who through addiction have lost
their health and freedom. Restore to them the assurance of your
unfailing mercy; remove from them the fears that beset them;
strengthen in the work of their recovery; and to those who
care for them, give patient understanding and persevering love.

Praise the Lord, O my soul,
and forget not all his benefits—
who forgives all your sins
and heals all your diseases,
who redeems your life from the pit
and crowns you with love and compassion. —Ps. 103:2–4 NIV

FELLOW TRAVELERS

Higher Power, who fills our whole life, and whose presence we
find wherever we go, preserve us who travel the road of recovery,
surround us with your loving care, protect us from every danger,
and bring us in safety to our journey's end.

The Lord bless you and keep you; the Lord make his face to shine upon
you and be gracious to you; the Lord turn his face toward you and give
you peace. —Num. 6:24–26 NIV

AN IRISH BLESSING

May the road rise to meet you,
May the wind be always at your back.

May the sun shine warm on your face,
The rain fall softly on your fields,

And until we meet again,
May God hold you in the palm of his hand.

*We always thank God, the Father of our Lord Jesus Christ, when we
pray for you.* —*Col. 1:3 NIV*

FOR THOSE WHO HAVE RELAPSED

O God of all mercies and comfort, who helps us in time of need,
we humbly ask you to behold, visit, and relieve those who have
relapsed, for whom our prayers are desired. Look upon them with
the eyes of your mercy; comfort them with a sense of your goodness;
preserve them from the temptations of their addiction; and give
them patience under their affliction. In your time, restore them to
the program and physical, mental, and spiritual health. And help
them, we pray, to listen, believe, and do your will.

*They refused to listen and failed to remember the miracles you per-
formed among them...but you are a forgiving God, gracious and compassionate, slow to anger and abounding in love. Therefore you did not
desert them.* —*Neh. 9:17 NIV*

MY PRAYER FOR YOU

I thought of you so much today
I went to God in prayer,
To ask him to watch over you
And show you that we care.

My prayer for you was not for rewards
That you could touch or feel,
But true rewards for happiness
That are so very real.

Like love and understanding
In all the things you do,
And guidance when you need it most
To see your troubles through.

I asked him for good health for you
So your future could be bright,
And faith to accept life's challenges
And the courage to do what's right.

I gave thanks to him for granting my prayer
To bring you peace and love.
May you feel the warmth in your life
With God's blessings from above.

May God himself, the God of peace, sanctify you through and through.
May your whole spirit, soul, and body be kept blameless at the coming of
our Lord Jesus Christ. —*1 Thess. 5:23 NIV*

THINGS TO GIVE

Today, I pray I may give:
To my enemy:	Forgiveness.
To my opponent:	Tolerance.
To my customer:	Service.
To a friend:	Kindness.
To all people:	Charity.
To my family:	My heart.
To every child:	A good example.
To myself:	Respect.
To you Higher Power:	*Love*

    With all my heart,
    With all my soul,
    With all my mind.

So in everything, do to others what you would have them do to you, for
this sums up the Law and the Prophets. —*Matt. 7:12 NIV*

LOVE

Higher Power, remind me that:
Love is patient;
Love is kind.
Love is not jealous; it does not put on airs; it is not snobbish.
Love is never rude; it is not self-seeking; it is not prone to anger;

neither does it brood over injuries.
Love does not rejoice in what is wrong, but rejoices with the truth.

There is no limit to love's forbearance, its truth, its hope, its power to endure.

Love the Lord your God with all your heart and with all your soul and with all your strength and with all your mind; and, Love your neighbor as yourself. —*Luke 10:27 NIV*

PRAYER OF SAINT FRANCIS OF ASSISI

Lord, make me an instrument of your peace!
Where there is hatred, let me sow love.
Where there is injury, pardon.
Where there is doubt, faith.
Where there is despair, hope.
Where there is darkness, light.
Where there is sadness, joy.
O Divine Master, grant that I may not so much seek
To be consoled as to console.
To be understood as to understand.
To be loved as to love.
For it is in giving that we receive.
It is in pardoning that we are pardoned.
It is in dying that we are born to eternal life.

"The Spirit of the Lord is on me, because he has anointed me to preach good news to the poor. He has sent me to proclaim freedom for the prisoners and recovery of sight for the blind, to release the oppressed, to proclaim the year of the Lord's favor." —*Luke 4:18–19 NIV*

DO THE RIGHT THING

Help me, Higher Power, to get out of myself, to stop always thinking what I need. Show me the way I can be helpful to others, and supply me with the strength to do the right thing.

A generous man will prosper; he who refreshes others will himself be refreshed. —*Prov. 11:25 NIV*

TOLERANCE PRAYER

Higher Power, help me to know the most lovable quality I can possess is tolerance. It is the vision that enables me to see things from another's viewpoint. It is the generosity that concedes to others the right to their own opinions and their own peculiarities. It is the bigness that enables me to let people be happy in their own way instead of my way.

You, then, why do you judge your brother? Or why do you look down on your brother? For we will all stand before God's judgment seat.
—*Rom. 14:10 NIV*

NOT MY PEOPLE

Dear Lord,

I went to a meeting today—not the meeting I usually attend.

The room was full of all sorts—not the group I usually mingle with.
The language was rather course—not the words I would have chosen.
The air was thick and blue—not the way I wanted my clothes to smell.
The stories were full of awful pain—not the sort of pain I've known.
The people were rough and broken—but their hearts were tender and warm.

Their struggles were overwhelming—but they spoke of provision and miracle.
They had scars and wounds from battles—but spoke of victories won.
They spoke of life's hardships—but extolled faith as the only real key.

Lord, these people were not my people—but somehow we were strangely one.
Keep them, heal them, meet their needs—bless them as they blessed me.

Accept one another, then, just as Christ accepted you, in order to bring praise to God. —*Rom. 15:7 NIV*

I CANNOT PRAY

I cannot pray the Lord's Prayer and even once say "I."
I cannot pray the Lord's Prayer and even once say "my."
Nor can I pray the Lord's Prayer and not pray for another,
And when I ask for daily bread, I must include my brother.
For others are included in each and every plea,
From the beginning to the end of it, it does not once say "me."

Be devoted to one another in brotherly love. Honor one another above yourselves. —*Rom. 12:10 NIV*

Chapter Ten

Prayers of Thanksgiving

Specific expressions of thanks related to God's deliverance, help, and provision.

Let them give thanks to the Lord for his unfailing love and his wonderful deeds for men.
                    —Psalm 107:8 NIV

*P*rayers of thanksgiving are prayerful expressions of gratitude to God. In the Old Testament, prayers of thanksgiving are usually quite specific and related to God's deliverance, help, and provision. Giving specific thanks is important in prayers of thanksgiving. If someone just says "Thanks!" to us, we are naturally curious to know why we are being thanked. God is no different.

When we pray prayers of thanks and mention our specific reasons for thankfulness, we remind ourselves of many things. We remember what it felt like to be in need. We recall that God can be trusted to answer prayer. We remind ourselves not to take God's provision for granted. And we recollect that we are not responsible for obtaining the blessing or answer—God is.

The Book of Psalms is replete with specific prayers of thanks. In fact, the Psalms provide a wonderful format for prayers of thanksgiving. The general form for a prayer/psalm of thanksgiving is as follows:

Present Blessedness: The psalmist describes how at present he is blessed and happy as a result of God's intervention, protection, deliverance, and so on. An up-to-date example might be, "Lord, I am finally straightened around. Thanks to your help, I'm at peace. I can even sleep again, and I'm not pacing the floor with anxiety."

Former Anguish: Next, the psalmist presents a poetic recollection of his former anguish. He describes with some detail the events that led him to call upon the Lord for help. For example, "I had really lost it for a while. I was overcome with fears. I thought my job was in jeopardy, and I was afraid my money wouldn't stretch. I felt so all alone, and I didn't think anybody cared. I believed I was too stupid and incompetent to deal with life. All I wanted to do was panic and escape."

Prayer for Deliverance: The psalmist then restates his prayer for help, and he repeats his desperate cry for deliverance. For example, "But in the midst of my panic attack, I cried out for your help, Lord. I felt like you were the only one I could talk to. I told you my fears, my crazy thoughts, and my insanity."

God's Deliverance: Then, the story of God's specific deliverance is told. Literary license is often taken by the psalmist as he depicts God coming with thunder and lightning, earthquakes, and terrors. It is always an exciting recollection of God's action on behalf of his people. We might then continue the prayer by saying, "After I had poured my heart out to you, your peace swept over me like a cool mist. Miraculously, I felt a release, I felt a heavy weight lifted off me. I knew in my heart somehow that you had made it all OK. Once I had given you my anxiety, you gave me your peace."

Praise and Thanks: Finally, praise and thanks are offered. For example, "Thank you, Lord, for your peace. Thank you for hearing my cry. Thank you for being so near. I love you, Lord!"

Take the time to read a few psalms of thanksgiving. Psalm 32 is a thanksgiving for forgiveness. Psalm 40 is a thanksgiving for faith and trust. Psalm 69 is a thanksgiving for deliverance from enemies. Psalm 130 is a thanksgiving for redemption and forgiveness.

What is the point in all this? Whereas it is OK to thank the Lord in general for the new day, the warm sun, a good spouse, a job, and so forth, our prayer relationship with God needs to mature and become dynamic. We have learned in the types of prayer how we can approach God in honest complaint, and we communicate with him in a manner similar to the communication we would have with any person. Therefore, he needs to be specifically thanked, as we would specifically thank a coworker, spouse, child, or neighbor.

Why not take the time to develop a meaningful and specific prayer of thanks? It may not take the flowery form of a psalm or poem, but it can assume the sincere and unfeigned form of a specific and thankful communication from our heart.

Although the following prayers don't all follow the form of a psalm/ prayer of thanksgiving, they are nevertheless examples of thanksgiving prayers. Let us learn from them and from the Psalms and develop a living, dynamic ability to thank God for his goodness to us.

Prayers of Thanksgiving

"TO BE" PRAYER

O Lord, I ain't what I ought to be,
And I ain't what I want to be,
And I ain't what I'm going to be,
But O Lord, I thank you
That I ain't what I used to be.

*And we . . . are being transformed into his likeness with ever increasing
glory, which comes from the Lord, who is the Spirit.*
                                                    —2 Cor. 7:18 NIV

FOR ANOTHER DAY

Thank you, dear God, for another day,
The chance to live in a decent way,
To feel again the joy of living,
And happiness that comes from giving.
Thank you for friends who can understand
And the peace that flows from your loving hand.
Help me to wake to the morning sun
With the prayer, "Today thy will be done,"
For with your help I will find the way.
Thank you again, dear God, for another day.

*This is the day which the Lord has made;
    let us rejoice and be glad it in.*   —Ps. 118:24 NIV

THANK YOU, GOD

Thank you, God, for all you have given me.
Thank you for all you have taken from me.
But, most of all, I thank you, God, for what you've left me:
Recovery, along with peace of mind, faith, hope, and love.

Let them give thanks to the Lord for his unfailing love
and his wonderful deeds for men. —Ps. 107:8 NIV

O GOD OF OUR UNDERSTANDING

This is the dawn of a new day in the program. I shall thank you, my Higher Power, for last night's rest, your gift.

Yesterday is gone, except for what I have learned from it, good and bad. Today, I have the same choice, a divine privilege that swells my heart with hope and purpose. This is my day, the purity of a new beginning.

I will receive from this day exactly what I give to it. As I do good things, good will be done to me. It is my gift to mold into something everlasting and do those things that will affect the people around me in an ever-winding circle. The worthiness of this effort rests entirely with me.

This is my day for love, because I know that as I love, I will be loved. Hate and jealousy cannot exist in the presence of love. I will be sustained by this miracle of your creation and this day will be lightened by my love for others and especially love for my fellow travelers in the program.

Today I will do my best without thought of failures of the past or anxieties for the future. When this day is ended I will have no regrets. On retiring I shall thank you, my Higher Power, for this wonderful day.

Be very careful, then, how you live—not as unwise but as wise, making
the most of every opportunity, because the days are evil.
—Ephes. 5:15–16 NIV

LANGUAGE OF THE HEART

Dear God,
You know my needs before I ask,
 my heart before I pray, and
 my gratitude before I even offer my thanks.
You understand me better than I understand myself,
 and I thank you for communicating with me in the
 language of the heart.

We do not know what we ought to pray for, but the Spirit himself
intercedes for us with groans that words cannot express.
            —Rom. 8:26b NIV

THE GRATITUDE PRAYER

O God,
. . . It is good to be able to get my feet on the floor again.
It is good to be able to do at least some things for myself again.
It is best of all just to have the joy of feeling well again.
O God,
Keep me grateful;
Grateful to all the people who helped me back to health;
Grateful to you for the way in which you have brought me
 through it all.
O God,
Still give me patience.
Help me not to be in too big a hurry to do too much.
Help me to keep on doing what I'm told to do.
Help me to be so obedient to those who know what is best for me
 that very soon I shall be on the top of the world and on the top
 of my job again.
I can say what the psalmist said:
I waited patiently for the Lord;
He inclined to me and heard my cry.
He took me from a fearful pit, and from the miry clay,
And on a rock he set my feet, establishing my way.

In my anguish I cried to the Lord, and he answered me by setting me free. —*Ps. 118:5 NIV*

TO CHANGE

I pray that I may continue to change, and
I appreciate you for investing in me your time, your patience, your
   understanding and for seeing in me someone worthwhile.
I am sorry for the past—but I will change for the better, and
I am grateful for the opportunity!

Not that I have already obtained all this, or have already been made perfect, but I press on to take hold of that for which Christ Jesus took hold of me. —*Phil. 3:12 NIV*

YOUR GIFT

Thank you, Higher Power, for your gift of recovery; through this program I have come to know myself better than ever before, and I have come to know others better as well. I pray that I may be eternally grateful for this, your blessing!

Thanks be to God for his indescribable gift! —*2 Cor. 9:15 NIV*

KINDNESS AND SERVICE

O Lord, help me always to remember thankfully the work of those who helped me when I needed help. Reward them for their kindness and service, and grant that I may have the will, the time, and the opportunity to do the same for others.

Because of the service by which you have proved yourselves, men will praise God for the obedience that accompanies your confession of the gospel of Christ, and for your generosity in sharing with them and with everyone else. —*2 Cor. 9:13 NIV*

ANNIVERSARY PRAYER

Dear God, I had another anniversary today, one more year in recovery. It has been difficult at times, but it has allowed many blessings.

I am a human being again. I feel new strength in my body, spirit, and mind. The world has never looked so good. I have my friends' and family's respect. I am productive in my work. I do not miss the slippery people and places. When I have been

tempted, you, my Higher Power, have sustained me. I have found a home in the fellowship, and friends support me. Stay close by me, God. I thank you. *This is the life I love.*

How great is your goodness,
  which you have stored up for those who fear you,
which you bestow in the sight of men
  on those who take refuge in you.   —*Ps. 31:19 NIV*

Chapter Eleven

Prayers of Praise

Expressions of our worship and adoration to God that focus on the person of God.

"Praise be to you, O Lord, God of our father Israel, from everlasting to everlasting ... Yours, O Lord, is the kingdom; you are exalted as head over all." —1 Chronicles 29:10-11 NIV

$\mathcal{P}$rayers of praise are expressions of worship and adoration to God. Unlike prayers of thanks, praise is unrelated to what God has done. Praise focuses on the person of God, not his blessings.

God created us humans for fellowship with himself. Among all the creatures of the world, humans alone were made for God and made in God's image. For this reason, humans are most fulfilled when they are in intimate fellowship with their creator. Praise is the best way to express that intimate fellowship.

Just as lovers share intimate communication with one another and speak words of unconditional love, God's people who were created for him are most fulfilled when they unconditionally express their love and adoration to him. In fact, God often likens his relationship with his people to the relationship between a bride and groom.

Unfortunately, our prayers and communications with God are usually filled with petitions instead of praises. Our petitions, like our thoughts, are often self-consumed. Our prayers are similar to our communications with others. For example, when we sit in a support group or a Twelve-Step meeting, we wonder what we should say next, and we wonder if our last comment was stupid. We want to be acknowledged but not scrutinized; we want to be recognized but not examined. We wonder what others are thinking of us, and we relate everything we hear to our own circumstances and problems. In the same way, our prayers are often filled with ourselves.

And when we do attempt praise, we often offer praises that are merely thanksgivings in disguise. We have all heard someone say, "I praise you, Lord, for giving me...(whatever)." That is a fine prayer, but it's thanksgiving, not praise. That's like looking into your lover's eyes as you sit before the roaring fireplace the then whispering tenderly, "Honey, I love you because you made great fried chicken tonight."

Praise is offered unconditionally and freely—the spontaneous response of a heart filled with love, not gratitude. A prayer of praise might say, "I love you, Lord. I praise your awesome might and creative majesty. You above all others are God—the lover of my soul." Praise is offered to God for who he is—for his character and being, not for his actions and grace in our behalf. Consider the romantic setting again. Except this time, we say, "My love, you are the only one I desire. I am captured by your tender ways. Above all others, you are the fairest and most precious. I love you."

Prayers of praise are important to those of us in recovery because, in order to mature, our relationship with God must transcend ourselves and our need of God (what he does for us). We must move to a place of seeing God's need. We among all people are first to recognize our need of God, but we must also be first to demonstrate that we understand God's need—a need only God's children can meet—the need to be loved.

God is, of course, self-sufficient. And he really needs no one or no thing. But can the one who created love and first showed it not desire to be loved in return? Saint John says, "We love because he [God] first loved us." (1 John 4:19 NIV)

Why do many of us have children? Do we think the world needs another soul or two? Do we want to bring another life into this wonderful place of struggle and survival and suffering? Do we want someone to carry on our name? Or do we want a little boy or girl with our eyes and grandma's nose? Little ones who wrap their arms around our neck and say, "I love you, Mommy."

A mother once noticed that her young daughter was upset with her doll. The girl cycled through a strange ritual as she first hugged her doll and then stared probingly into the painted and plastic face. Finally, the little girl shook her doll.

"What's wrong with your baby?" the mothers inquired. The tiny daughter somberly spoke as her bottom lip protruded, "Mommy, I love her and I love her, but she never loves me back." As our relationship with God matures, we learn to love him back.

To stay dynamic and alive, we need to be willing to change, mature, develop, and grow. And in our relationship with our Higher Power, the best indicator of a dynamic and maturing relationship is the presence of praise, the unconditional loving response of our hearts to God. Saint Augustine said, "God is not greater if you reverence him, but you are greater if you serve [praise] him."

Biblical psalms of praise are numerous. Psalms 8 and 19 respond to God's wondrous presence and majesty in creation. Psalm/prayers of joy in adoration are found in Psalms 95 through 100. Psalms 111 through 118 are festive celebration psalm/prayers. Like the celebration of love at a marriage, the Jews knew how to celebrate their love for God. Many festivals and feasts filled the Jewish calendar, but only one day of mandatory fasting. Finally, Psalms 146 through 150 are the "Great Hallels," the Great Praises.

Prayers of praise are often the most difficult for us to pray. Just as the married couple who take one another for granted find it hard to express their love, we can grow cold in our concern for God himself. We can lose sight of our original purpose in creation. It is healthy for us to look beyond ourselves, and the expression of praise and adoration to God is a good place to start. Someone once said, "If God is kept on the outside, something is wrong on the inside."

The following psalms and prayers of praise can be used as tools to develop our own praise to God. They remind us that we can do more than just speak words of adoration and love to God—we can sing, play instruments, dance, and so on. When we praise God without thanking him for some benefit, we focus on his majesty, his greatness, and his intrinsic worth.

Prayers of Praise

Praise the Lord.
Sing to the Lord a new song,
  his praise in the assembly of the saints.
Let Israel rejoice in their Maker;
  let the people of Zion be glad in their King.
Let them praise his name with dancing
  and make music to him with tambourine and harp [guitar].
For the lord takes delight in his people;
  he crowns the humble with salvation.
Let the saints rejoice in this honor
  and sing for joy on their beds.
May the praise of God be in their mouths...
  Praise the Lord.
                                                —Ps. 149:1–6 NIV

Praise the Lord.
Praise God in his sanctuary;
  praise him in his mighty heavens.
Praise him for his acts of power;
  praise him for his surpassing greatness.
Praise him with the sounding of the trumpet,
  praise him with the harp and lyre,
praise him with tambourine and dancing,
  praise him with the strings and flute,
praise him with the clash of cymbals,
  praise him with resounding cymbals.
Let everything that has breath praise the Lord.
Praise the Lord.
                                                —Ps. 150 NIV

DAVID'S LAST PRAYER OF PRAISE TO GOD

Praise be to you, O Lord, God of our father Israel,
  from everlasting to everlasting.
Yours, O Lord, is the greatness and the power
  and the glory and the majesty and the splendor,
  for everything in heaven and earth is yours.
Yours, O Lord, is the kingdom;
  you are exalted as head over all.
Wealth and honor come from you;
  you are the ruler of all things.
In your hands are strength and power
  to exalt and give strength to all.
Now, our God, we...praise your glorious name.
                              —1 Chron. 29:10–13 NIV

I LOVE YOU LORD

I love you Lord and
I lift my voice
To worship you.
Oh my soul rejoice.

Take joy my king
In what you hear.
Let me be a sweet,
Sweet sound
In your ears.

Now to the King eternal, immortal, invisible, the only God, be honor
and glory for ever and ever. Amen,   *—1 Tim. 1:17* NIV

WORTHY OF MY PRAISE

Heavenly Father,
Whenever I look into the sky at night,
   I am overwhelmed by your greatness.
Whenever I consider the human body,
   I am amazed at your designs.
Whenever I ponder the wisdom of your word,
   I am reminded of your plans.
Whenever I experience the warmth of a friend,
   I am touched by your heart.
Whenever I see the way of a mother with her babe,
   I am told of your tenderness.
Whenever I ponder life itself,
   I am humbled by your power.
You are great and worthy of my praise.

*I praise you because I am fearfully and wonderfully made; your works
are wonderful, I know that full well.*   —Ps. 139:14 NIV

WHAT CAN I SAY?

Dear Lord,

What can I say to the One who made my life?
How can the vessel give praise to the potter?
Why would the creator want to even hear from me?

Before I speak, you already know my thought.
When I offer praise, you've heard it before.
If I were to sing, I could never match heaven.

I feel so small, I'd rather not try.
I have no special words to form praise, anyway
My words hit the ceiling and bounce back.

But just when I decided not to even try,
I noticed a bird just outside my window.
He sang and he sang with all of his might.
I couldn't help wonder that such a large voice

Came from such a small creature as he.
Then, Lord, I found new eyes and ears.

I heard the bird speaking, "Glory to Your name!"
He cried out to the heavens,
"Praise God, my Maker, my Provider, my Life!"

I watched his song rise like incense.
It ascended like a fragrance to your presence.
And I watched you close your eyes, smile, and inhale.

But it was only a bird who spoke, who sang.
It was just a tiny creature, barely worth notice.
Yet you heard, you received—you were pleased.

What can I say to the one who made my life?
I can say, "Glory to your name, O God of my life.
Here is my voice returned and lifted in praise."

"Are not two sparrows sold for a penny? Yet not one of them will fall to the ground apart from the will of your Father."

—*Matt. 10:29* NIV

Chapter Twelve

The Practice of Prayer

Pray without ceasing.

"But when you pray, go into your room, close the door and pray to your Father, who is unseen. Then your Father, who sees what is done in secret, will reward you." —Matthew 6:6 NIV

*T*he preceding chapters instruct us how to pray. The practice of prayer is the practical application of that instruction and knowledge. Many people today talk about developing a daily one-hour prayer discipline and encourage believers to do so. It is a wonderful idea, but we in recovery want a lifetime and a lifestyle of prayer and communion with God, not just an hour a day. Although it seems impossible, the Bible encourages believers to "pray without ceasing."

When we are told to develop certain prayer disciplines, many of us offer resistance. The sound of regimen, discipline, rules, and directives can rub us the wrong way. We've learned to live by slogans such as "Easy Does It," "Let Go and Let God," and "Go With the Flow." For us, the practice of prayer needs to be a free flow of communication to a person: God. And like communication with a person, prayer must be multi-dimensional and dynamic—a living connection.

Although prayer is vital to every step in the program, Step Eleven is most often thought of in the context of prayer. Step Eleven states that we are to use prayer and meditation as a means to improve our conscious contact with God. Brother Lawrence, a seventeenth-century monk who served his monastery as cook, coined the phrase "practicing the presence of God" (see the book by that title: *Practicing the Presence of God* by Brother Lawrence). That is exactly the goal of Step Eleven prayer: to improve and maintain our conscious contact with God—to practice his presence continually. That is our ultimate goal in prayer.

In order to accomplish quality prayer time, we set aside times and places for prayer. With that in mind, let us search our hearts, our daily routines, and our houses for a time and place for prayer. The daily appointments we make and keep with God will provide the foundation and training for a lifestyle of prayer.

If we employ all of the types and elements of prayers that we have discussed, our prayer and communication with God can be dynamic, realistic, and sincere. Just as a student learning a foreign language has to be brave enough to try out new phrases and expressions in order to develop the ability to speak the new language, we use the various types of prayer to develop a breadth and depth to our prayer-life.

USING THE TYPES OF PRAYER AS A GUIDE

The various types of prayer are useful to developing a guideline for prayer.

Petition: We can begin our prayer time by asking God for specific knowledge of his will for us and for the power to carry that out. Then we can pray other more specific petitions that we know are in line with his will—petitions with a higher purpose.

Declaration: Next we can report to God about our lives. When Mom asked us, "What did you do at school today?" we always had a lot to report. In the same way we imagine that God is asking, "So what's going on in your life?" he already knows, of course, but he delights to hear our report, our declaration.

Complaint: A declaration will undoubtedly bring us to a place of complaint before God. Now we can tell him where it hurts and how our lives stink at times. We can pour our hearts out to him, knowing that he will not judge us or condemn us because we are being honest about our feelings.

Meditation: Next, we practice meditative prayer or listening prayer. We take time to quiet our hearts, disengage our minds, awaken our spirits, and invite God's Holy Spirit to pray through us according to God's will for our lives.

Submission: Having prayed for knowledge of God's will, having prayed according to God's will, having reported to God about our life, having complained about our hurts and problems, and having practiced listening prayer, we are now ready to submit in prayer to God. Like Jesus, who struggled with the Father's will in the Garden of Gethsemane, we have sought God's will, struggled with it, and finally submitted to it in prayer.

Penitent: In prayers of penitence we come to God asking him to search our hearts for sins and defects. We express our remorse for the sins he shows us. We specifically confess those defects and faults. We repent of them with a change of mind, heart, and attitude. Finally, we humbly pray for God's mercy and forgiveness—the removal of our shortcomings and sins.

Imprecatory: Having identified our own personal sins and defects, we find it easier to specifically identify the enemies that assail our lives. We now bring those enemies to God's attention and ask him to defeat them.

Intercession: Our thoughts and our prayers begin to turn away from ourselves as we conclude with three types of prayer that are centered on others: intercession, thanks, and praise. In intercession, we pray for others by first asking for God's will to be revealed in their lives. Then, we pray for those that we know are in accordance with God's will for them.

Thanksgiving: We now pray prayers of thanksgiving for specific blessings and the goodness of God in our lives. Although it is good to thank him in general, we take the time to specifically recall his goodness and tell God how grateful we are for it.

Praise: In an ultimate break from self-consideration, we express our love and adoration for God. We praise him not for what he has done, but we praise him for who he is. We extol his might, his majesty, his creative glory, his awesome power. Just as lovers would exchange loving words of praise for one another's character and beauty, we express our love and admiration to God.

WORKING THE TYPES OF PRAYER

Just as one might "work the steps," we can also learn to "work the elements of prayer." The following is an example of working the types of prayer on a specific issue or problem. The person praying below is unemployed.

Lord, I came outside to walk around the block with you and talk. I know you've probably been waiting to hear from me today, but being unemployed keeps me pretty busy reading the paper, making calls, writing letters, doing interviews, and stuff. Most of the time I want to get upset and worry, but I know that's when it's time to pray. So here I am.

Although I feel vulnerable praying this, Lord, I do want to know what your will for me is. I know that you know what job I should have, and I also know that you can show me. Please do. And once you do show me your will, give me the power to do what you're asking of me. Help me to carry out your plan. And if you're going to ask me to take some risks or try something new, I'll need courage, too. *(Petition for God's Will)*

Because I'm out of work right now, God, I need the money to pay my rent and provide food – but you already know that. Jesus said not to worry about those things because God knows our needs and is willing to supply them. So please help me. I know you want me to work, I know you want me to provide for my family, I know you want me to feel like a contributing member of society; so please, God, give me a job. Do what I haven't been able to do for myself. Open a door for me somewhere. *(Other Petitions)*

I'm not panicky about this unemployment. My family and I have our health, I'm not disabled or insane (although I feel like it at times), we still have our friends, and the car is working again. I remember how your word in the Bible says that you know my needs. Your promise is to feed and clothe us like the sparrows and the flowers of the field. I just hope you never forget that promise. Apart from the fact that the money is running out, I guess everything is okay—maybe tolerable. *(Prayer of Declaration)*

But, Lord, I'm not sure how long it will all stay OK. I may not be in a panic, but I do have fear lurking just under my skin. My wife is the one in a full panic attack. She worries me. I feel so damned guilty. But I didn't get fired—just laid off. It happens to everybody these days. I feel so worthless. Hurry, God, I'm tired of waiting for you. I wonder sometimes if you even care, or if you hear. *(Prayer of Complaint)*

(He quietly sings a little familiar song he learned as a child. He sings it over and over until a wave of peace and God's presence floods his heart. He feels the deepest hurts and cries of his heart being poured out through the simple melody. He feels accepted, comforted. He weeps.) *(Prayer of Meditation)*

God, I know that you love me and that you do have a plan for me. Although I don't like this time of waiting, I'm just going to entrust my life to you somehow. I want your plan, I want your will. Give me serenity to accept what I can't change—I can't change or hurry you. I want you to have your way in my life. *(Prayer of Submission)*

Lord, I want to draw closer to you and I want to submit more fully to you, but I know that there are still things in my life that keep me too distant from you and others. Show me what's wrong inside me. I'm still so filled with doubt—doubt about your reality and your goodness. I'm sorry for doubting you. I confess my lack of faith. I really want it removed. Forgive me, please. I'm also filled with hateful anger. I'm so damned angry at everyone: my kids, the mailman, the dog, everybody. And I guess I'm angry at you. Sorry. *(Prayer of Penitence)*

Inside of me, Lord, there are some pretty ugly monsters that have ruled me for years. They wake up with me and follow me through my day. They tell me how stupid I am. They sound just like my dad, who told me I was worthless and wouldn't amount to anything. They're keeping me unemployed, God. I can't even try to feel good about myself or present myself to others so long as these monsters torment me. Please, God, destroy them—silence them. Cut out their tongues; muzzle their condemning voices. *(Prayer of Imprecation)*

I can't imagine what my being without a job has done to my wife inside. Please help her, Lord. And bless my kids. Make this

Christmas special somehow, even though they won't have the gifts or stuff they've had before. Make up for it in some other way. Okay, God? *(Prayer of Intercession)*

You have been good to me during this time, Lord, even though I focus on the bad stuff. I don't want to be ungrateful. When the car was making that noise and I was afraid it was real bad, I prayed for your help. You sent George over from the Tuesday group to look at it. He even had the stuff to fix it—we never even had to buy a part. Thanks for taking care of us that day. *(Prayer of Thanksgiving)*

It's pretty cold out here now, but your stars sure are beautiful. If you're anything like your universe, you must be pretty awesome. I love you, God. I'm not saying that to manipulate you into some favor or to get on your good side. I just want you to know that I think you're great. You're so big, and yet I really know in my heart that I'm special to you—I'm loved. So right back at you, Lord—I love you. *(Prayer of Praise)*

ORDER FORM ❋ RPI PUBLISHING

Name

Address

City	State	Zip

Phone (   )　　　　　**Email**

Code	Title	Price	Qty	Total
1443	The Twelve Steps - A Spiritual Journey (ASJ)	$18.95		
1575	The Twelve Steps for Christians	$14.95		
1214	Meditations for the Twelve Steps ASJ	$12.95		
1281	Prayers for the Twelve Steps ASJ	$12.95		
1117	The 12 Steps - A Way Out	$18.95		
PDF	12 Step Prayers for a Way Out (PDF version)	$ 7.95		
1125	The 12 Steps For Adult Children	$12.95		
1354	The 12 Steps-A Guide for Adults With ADD	$12.95		
1584	Tending the Soul	$12.95		

Shipping & Handling Charges

ship via	$0-30	$31-50	Mark your shipping selection	
Media Mail*	$3.00	$6.00	○	**SUBTOTAL**
UPS Standard	$10.50	$15.00	○	CA residents add 8% sales tax
UPS 3 Day	$20.00	$30.00	○	Shipping (see chart) Grnd Shipping FREE on orders over $50*
UPS 2 Day	$30.00	$40.00	○	
*takes 7-14 days				

Call us for discounts on quantities of 5+ books
800-873-8384　　　**TOTAL**

Visa & MasterCard Accepted

Card No. _____　Exp. Date _____

Signature _____　CVC Code _____

Make checks payable to RPI Publishing, Inc.
Mailing address: PO Box 66398, Scotts Valley, CA 95067

Go to our website at rpipublishing.com *to order online and view additional items, including recovery books, cards, card-packs and posters.*